MATH FUNDAMENTALS FOR AUDIO

THE COMPUTER MUSIC AND DIGITAL AUDIO SERIES

John Strawn, Founding Editor
James Zychowicz, Series Editor

Recent titles include:

New Digital Musical Instruments: Control and Interaction Beyond the Keyboard
Eduardo R. Miranda and
  Marcelo M. Wanderley, with a
  Foreword by Ross Kirk

Fundamentals of Digital Audio
New Edition
Alan P. Kefauver and David Patschke

Hidden Structure: Music Analysis Using Computers
David Cope

A-Life for Music Music and Computer Models of Living Sysems
Eduardo Reck Miranda

Designing Audio Objects for Max/MSP and Pd
Eric Lyon

The Art and Technique of Electroacoustic Music
Peter Elsea

Math Fundamentals for Audio
Leslie Gaston-Bird

Volume 27 • THE COMPUTER MUSIC AND DIGITAL AUDIO SERIES

MATH FUNDAMENTALS FOR AUDIO

Leslie Gaston-Bird

With a Chapter by Jamie Angus-Whiteoak

Illustrations by Andrew M. Whiteoak

Middleton, Wisconsin

To Andrew Lenard

 ISBN 978-0-89579-837-4

A-R Editions, Inc., Middleton, Wisconsin 53562
© 2020 All rights reserved
Printed in the United States of America

10 8 6 4 2 1 3 5 7 9

Contents

Acknowledgments	viii
List of Figures	ix
A Word to Instructors	xiii
Introduction	1
Chapter One Basic Math Review	**7**
Using a Calculator	7
Finding Logarithms with a Calculator	7
Finding Trigonometric Values with a Calculator	8
The Inverse Function and Inverse Relationships	17
The Inverse Function and Simple Circuits	18
Calculating Delay Times Using Pro Tools	27
A Word on Latency	30
Working with Data Rates	34
Chapter Two Audio and Algebra	**37**
"Alphabet Soup" of Audio: Symbols and Terms	37
Cross Multiplication	39
Distance, Rate, Time, Wavelength, and Frequency	41
Calculating Wavelengths and Frequencies	42
Calculating Delay Times Using Algebra	49
Calculating Beats per Minute and Delay	54
Direct Current and Ohm's Law	56
Power Equations	57

Alternating Current   58
    Impedance of an Inductor   59
    Impedance of a Capacitor   60
    Capacitors in Audio Circuits   61
    Inductors in Audio Circuits   64
    Resonant Circuits   66
    The Analog Sound   66

Chapter Three   Audio and Logarithms   67
Ratios   67
Compression Ratios   67
Decibels   71
Power versus Voltage (Logarithms and Exponents)   71
    Antilogs   73
    The VU Problem   74
Powers of Two and Binary Numbers   76

Chapter Four   Reading Graphs   81
Locating Coordinates   81
Graphing Functions
    Cartesian Graphs   83
    Linear Graphs   86
    Polar Graphs   89

Chapter Five   Audio and Geometry   93
Geometry of a Circle   93
Geometry of a Sphere   94
Sound Propagation and Intensity: The Inverse Square Law   95
Working with Volume   96
The Geometric Mean   97

Chapter Six   Audio and Trigonometry   103
Sine and Cosine   103
The Unit Circle   104
Angular Velocity   105

Chapter Seven Audio and Calculus — 109
RMS — 109
Deriving Signal-to-Noise Ratio of a PCM System — 111
    An Advanced Look at Signal-to-Noise Ratio — 111
        The Signal — 111
        The Error — 113
    Error and Probability Density Function — 113
        Signal to Error — 116

Chapter Eight The Fourier Transform — 119
(by Jamie Angus-Whiteoak)

Fourier's Theorem — 119
Frequency Spectrum — 122
Fourier Analysis — 123
Frequency Analysis of Nonperiodic Signals:
  The Fourier Transform — 124
A Fourier Transform Example: The Single Pulse — 125

Chapter Nine Conclusion: Connecting Components — 129

Appendix A Metric Prefixes — 131

Appendix B Solutions to the Exercises — 133

Bibliography — 141

Index — 143

Acknowledgments

This book is dedicated to Andrew Lenard, my analytic geometry and calculus professor at Indiana University, Bloomington, who saw promise in my abilities and encouraged me to pursue a math major. Although I chose audio technology and telecommunications instead, I was honored.

This is also dedicated to Wayne Jackson and David Pickett for nurturing my love of audio at Indiana University and to the loving memory of my graduate school mentors and dear friends at the University of Colorado at Denver, the late Professor Roy Pritts and the late Professor Rich Sanders.

I am also grateful to my parents, who chose a Montessori education for me. I remember enjoying the binomial and trinomial cubes and magic zeroes. I believe that learning math without the pressure of grading prevented me from being intimidated by the subject.

Special thanks also to Dan Koetting, LeeAnn Weller, Ryan Gardner Smith, Mike Cramp, David Glasser, René Fancher, and MaryJane Wilcox.

A very special thanks to my husband, Andy Bird, who always helps me with basic addition and subtraction.

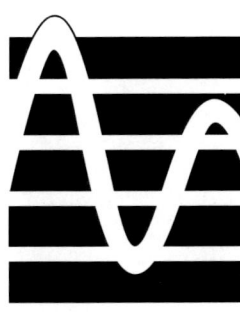

List of Figures

Chapter 1

Figure 1.1	Calculating the log of 2
Figure 1.2	Graph of $y = \sin(x)$
Figure 1.3	Switching between radians (a) and degrees (b)
Figure 1.4	Graph with x-axis shown in degrees
Figure 1.5	Graph with x-axis shown in radians
Figure 1.6	Sine function in radians
Figure 1.7	Sine π on a calculator.
Figure 1.8	Sine function in degrees
Figure 1.9	Sine 180° on a calculator
Figure 1.10	When your calculator is in the wrong mode
Figure 1.11	What one radian looks like
Figure 1.12	Calculating $\sin(2\pi)$
Figure 1.13	6 dB boost at 200 Hz, $Q = 10$
Figure 1.14	Three resistors in parallel
Figure 1.15	$1/100 = 0.01$
Figure 1.16	Press "M+"
Figure 1.17	Press "AC," display reads "0"
Figure 1.18	$1/200 = 0.005$
Figure 1.19	Press "M+"
Figure 1.20	$1/300 = 0.003$
Figure 1.21	Press "M+"
Figure 1.22	Press "AC," display reads "0"
Figure 1.23	Sum of values held in memory
Figure 1.24	Final answer: the inverse of 0.018
Figure 1.25	Vintage Pro Tools screen shot showing delay between stage mics (upper tracks) and house mics (lower tracks)

Figure 1.26   Pro Tools with time selected
Figure 1.27   Pro Tools screen showing delay caused by plug-in
Figure 1.28   The same track showing audio shifted 4,096 samples to the right

Chapter 2
Figure 2.1   A scale showing two sides of a balanced equation
Figure 2.2   The scale is unbalanced when a term is moved
Figure 2.3   The scale is balanced again when "like" terms are used on both sides
Figure 2.4   A car is used to illustrate wavelength
Figure 2.5   Two loudspeakers at different distances from the source
Figure 2.6   A triangle showing the equation $d = rt$
Figure 2.7   Cover the desired term with your finger to see the equation
Figure 2.8   Wristwatch with seconds and beats
Figure 2.9   A simple DC circuit
Figure 2.10   Alternating current and direct current
Figure 2.11   AC circuit with one inductor
Figure 2.12   AC circuit with one capacitor
Figure 2.13   Elephant
Figure 2.14   Mouse
Figure 2.15   Capacitor in series with audio signal (diagram made using CircuitLab.com)
Figure 2.16   High pass filter created with capacitor in series (diagram made using CircuitLab.com)
Figure 2.17   Capacitor in parallel with audio signal (diagram made using CircuitLab.com)
Figure 2.18   Low pas
Figure 2.19   Inductor in series with audio signal
Figure 2.20   Low pass filter created with an inductor in series (diagram made using CircuitLab.com)
Figure 2.21   Inductor in parallel with audio signal (diagrams made using CircuitLab.com)

Chapter 3
Figure 3.1   Pro Tools Compressor with ratio set to 1:1
Figure 3.2   Pro Tools Compressor with 2:1 ratio

Figure 3.3	Graphs of $y = x$, $y = x/2$, and $y = 2 + (x/2)$
Figure 3.4	Pro Tools Compressor with 10:1 ratio
Figure 3.5	A VU Meter

Chapter 4

Figure 4.1	Graph of the point (1,1)
Figure 4.2	Blank graph
Figure 4.3	The graph $y = 2$
Figure 4.4	The graph $y = x$
Figure 4.5	The graph $y = 3x$
Figure 4.6	The graph $y = 2 + 3x$
Figure 4.7	A linear graph showing car sales at a single dealership
Figure 4.8	A linear graph showing thousands of cars sold nationwide
Figure 4.9	Linear graph: a typical waveform display
Figure 4.10	Linear graph: a fundamental frequency and its harmonics
Figure 4.11	A logarithmic display used in an EQ
Figure 4.12	Speakers placed around a microphone at various angles
Figure 4.13	Polar plot showing 2 different frequency responses of a microphone
Figure 4.14	Linear plot showing 2 different frequency responses of a microphone

Chapter 5

Figure 5.1	The radius and circumference of a circle
Figure 5.2	Sound decreases by 6.02 dB as distance is doubled
Figure 5.3	The volume of a cuboid
Figure 5.4	A peak filter showing an f_c of 200 Hz and a Q of 10
Figure 5.5	Arithmetic and geometric means represented on a logarithmic graph
Figure 5.6	A peak filter with an f_c of 3,000 Hz and a Q of 2

Chapter 6

Figure 6.1	A way to visualize sine and cosine
Figure 6.2	The unit circle
Figure 6.3	A car travels along a sine wave
Figure 6.4	A sine wave with a frequency of 2 Hz
Figure 6.5	Finding the radius using Cartesian coordinates

Chapter 7

Figure 7.1	Sine wave with points highlighted at $\pi/2$, π, $3\pi/2$, and 2π
Figure 7.2	Viewing quantization levels on a 3-bit scale
Figure 7.3	A 4-bit system showing errors in aligning with the original waveform
Figure 7.4	Integration line

Chapter 8

Figure 8.1	The effect of adding four harmonically related sine waves together
Figure 8.2	The effect of adding four harmonically related cosine waves together
Figure 8.3	The frequency spectrum of the waveforms shown in Figures 8.1 and 8.2
Figure 8.4	A single rectangular pulse of length τ and amplitude of $\frac{1}{\tau}$
Figure 8.5	The spectrum of a single rectangular pulse of length τ for different values of τ

Appendix B

Figure B.2	The graph of $y = x/2$
Figure B.3	The graph of $y = x/10$

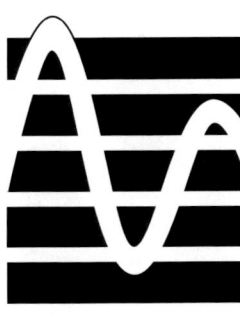

A Word to Instructors

At a few education forums held at Audio Engineering Society conferences, educators (most often from the United States) have complained that incoming recording arts students often lack basic math skills. This deficiency can prevent a student from succeeding in theory-based audio classes.

Just about every equation in this book is covered in US high schools, but for some reason some students have (1) not retained this information, (2) never learned it in the first place, or even (3) chose to disregard it during those years.

Could it be that studying music recording is seen as the "easy way out"? Perhaps it is a surprise to students that math really is everywhere and will rear its ugly head when it's time to study software like Pro Tools or record a drum kit (for example, time alignment of the snare with the overheads)!

This book is meant to serve as a companion to the textbooks on music recording already available. The goals of this book are:

- To bolster basic math skills that are necessary for understanding audio theory
- To present an easy-to-read approach that takes the intimidation factor out of textbooks (especially ones that make constant reference to math equations and assume basic math knowledge)
- To provide practical examples of solving problems specific to sound recording.

Reading this book should help students keep up with their textbooks in studio classes, even if all they want to do is "make beats," create music with Ableton, or engage in other laptop-based, solo music-making enterprises.

# Introduction

What does math have to do with recording music? Audio technology is all about *interconnectivity*, and so is math. As soon as your sound hits the analog-to-digital converter (ADC), every process that runs in the computer is a mathematical one. Wouldn't you like to know what's going on in that box?

I love math, but my strengths are in problem solving, not simple addition. I have to think a little too hard on simple problems—like, Quick! What is 35 plus 7?—or how to split the bill at a restaurant when out with friends.

Still, I love logic problems and making connections, and that is a great thing for an audio engineer. Whether it's routing a digital clock, making connections between an outboard compressor and a console, or getting from a laptop computer's stereo mini jack on stage to a live sound rig at the FOH (front of house): as audio engineers, we have to determine lots of ways to connect devices—and often very quickly!

Connecting mathematical concepts is also fun. I once saw a table of coefficients in a manual describing surround-sound downmixing, and I got excited when I saw the number 0.707. I knew, based on my experiences, that multiplying by 0.707 would reduce whatever input by 3 dB, and I was able to look at the coefficients for each channel and know the resulting attenuation. It was a *Matrix* moment for me, both because of the Hollywood film reference and because it's an actual matrix.

(Left Total) = 1.0L + 0.707C − 0.707S ;
(Right Total) = 1.0L + 0.707C + 0.707S ;

I don't even see the code any more. All I see is left at unity, center +3 dB, surround -3 dB, etc.

In the course of writing this book, I asked a few entertainment industry professionals why math is important. Here are some of my favorite responses:

> "As soon as your audio hits the computer, it is subjected to all sorts of mathematical computations."
>
> —*David Glasser, Airshow Mastering*

> "My favorite math equation to share with students is the rate of acceleration due to gravity: 9.8 m/s^2. That's how fast these 2-ton lighting ballasts will fall on you if you don't properly rig them."
> —Daniel Koetting, Associate Professor, University of Colorado Denver

> "When we were building these studios we had to know how to calculate wavelengths. It helps to know where standing waves are, and that the lowest frequencies are the size of this 50-foot long hallway."
> —Mike Cramp, Post Modern Company

> "You have to know percentages when dealing with performing contracts."
> —LeeAnn Weller, Former Events Manager, University of Colorado Denver

It helps to know that you are actually going to use this stuff during the course of your career after high school and college. Audio engineering and music production are such popular careers right now, and the competition is fierce. Why not give yourself a competitive edge? Being articulate about math will really impress your next client or employer!

Both acoustic sounds and electronic audio have a lot to do with circles and spheres (sound propagation), so you need geometry and trigonometry. Making sounds louder or softer is based on logarithmic addition and subtraction. Digital audio has everything to do with binary numbers, and even calculus is used to describe signal-to-error ratio. And of course, fractions are everywhere.

As an educator in the field of recording arts, I have taught hundreds of students various skills in audio production, including music recording, surround-sound recording, and post-production. I have always been surprised at how intimidated some students become when they have to solve seemingly simple, audio-related math problems. For example:

> *Problem: How many milliseconds of delay is caused by a plug-in that shows a 4 sample latency (based on a sampling frequency of 48 kHz)?*

When solving these kinds of very relevant, everyday problems, a few of my students make mistakes, some do not seem to be trying, and others don't even know where to begin. My conversations with these students reveal that they are excited about learning the math, but have always been challenged by it. It's rare to find students who don't seem to care at all. I love it when students try to help each other out with different ways of thinking about the problem. This is one of the best ways to learn—get help from your friends and think about the problem in a new way.

Whatever challenges you might face as a reader of this text, my aim is simply to show why math is crucial to understanding concepts in audio. Certainly there are various software programs and affordable smartphone apps to solve everyday audio problems: SPL meters, real-time analyzers, room-mode calculators, and more. But somewhere along the way, if you *truly* want to understand how to control and manipulate sound—and if you want to outshine the competition—you should learn some of the math behind the music.

HOW TO USE THIS BOOK

You will the following images throughout this book:

 **Clue: We found a magic number**

When you see this, you'll know that the number will appear again in future sections where I deal with more advanced concepts. "Magic numbers" are based on a lecture I give in which I begin by showing how sine waves relate to RMS (root mean squared) values, and how that in turn relates to signal-to-noise error and its corresponding "6 dB per bit" approximation. Seeing values such as 0.707, 1.414, 3 dB, and 6 dB come up again and again is pretty magical. You'll see why as you read along. The last chapter briefly summarizes these concepts.

 **More to Know**

If you are ready for a few more advanced ideas, continue reading through these sections.

 **Connecting Components**

These indicate sections where you can see how concepts fit together and try your hand at solving exercises.

A WORD ABOUT "MATH ANXIETY"

In her online course "How to Learn Math: For Students," Jo Boaler of Stanford University presents some myths about math.[1] I believe it is important for you to understand that if you have anxiety about learning math, you are not alone. Here are some highlights from her course:

1. It is a myth that math relies on memorization: it does not.
2. Your gender does not predetermine your ability to succeed at math.
3. Keeping a positive attitude is imperative—you can do it!
4. Making mistakes helps you to learn. If you are working your way through a maze, you will bump into walls. If you do the maze a second time, you learn what to avoid.
5. There is more than one way to solve a problem (especially in audio!).

NOTES

1. Jo Boaler, "How to Learn Math: For Students," Stanford Online, 2014, accessed 6 September 2016, https://lagunita.stanford.edu/courses/Education/EDUC115-S/Spring2014/about.

SELF-ASSESSMENT: IS THIS BOOK FOR YOU?

In order to find out whether you'll get any use out of this book, answer "yes" or "no" to the following questions:

Question:	Yes	No
1. I know a reference for the speed of sound in m/s (meters per second) or ft/s (feet per second). (See pp. 42–43: The speed of sound as a product of wavelength and frequency.)		
2. I know how to find the wavelength of a sine wave if given the frequency. (See pp. 44–45: The speed of sound as a product of wavelength and frequency.)		
3. If I know the beats per minute (bpm) of a song, I can determine how to create an echo or delay (in milliseconds) that matches the tempo. (See p. 55: Converting beats per minute to beats per second.)		
4. If I know the distance from a sound source, I can calculate the delays needed for a speaker array. (See pp. 52–54: A way to find delay times using only distance and speed of sound.)		
5. Given a peak value for a signal, I can find the RMS (root mean squared) value. (See p. 111: Finding the RMS value of a signal.)		
6. Given three or more resistors in parallel, I can find the total resistance represented by those three resistors in a simplified circuit. (See pp. 18–19: Finding the total resistance (RT) for resistors in parallel.)		
7. I can create a polar plot by measuring voltage values recorded from various positions in front of a microphone. (See figure 4-13.)		
8. Given the bandwidth, I can find the Q of an eq curve. (See p. 18: Q and bandwidth.)		
9. Given the impedance and peak voltage, I can find the power output by an amplifier. (See pp. 57–58.)		
10. Given a voltage, I can find a value that is 3 dB lower. (See p. 73: Computing the antilog of a number.)		
11. I know how to determine the signal to noise ratio of a system. (See Chapter 7, "An Advanced Look at Signal-to-Noise Ratio," p. 111.)		
12. I can determine the data rate for five tracks of audio recorded at 48 kHz, 24 bit. (See chapter 1, "Working with Data Rates," p. 34.)		
13. If 3 faders are set to "unity" on an analog console, and each has a sine wave corresponding to 0 VU when soloed, I can predict the VU value when all three are summed together. (See pp. 75–76: "Calculating dB using a VU meter".)		

If you answered "no" to 6 or more questions, you will probably find this book useful.

If you answered "no" to 3–5 questions, you might just want to peruse the more advanced sections.

If you answered "no" to fewer than 2 questions, then you probably do not need this book, but it could be a useful refresher.

ONE
Basic Math Review

USING A CALCULATOR

Let's start with something simple: basic operations on a calculator. You can use your smartphone or computer as long as its calculator has a scientific mode. (Sometimes you can find this by rotating the smartphone's screen so that you are looking at it in "landscape mode.")

Make sure your calculator has the following buttons:

- sin
- cos
- $1/x$
- 10^x
- DEG
- RAD
- $\log_{10}$

Finding Logarithms with a Calculator

For example,

Problem: "What is the base 10 logarithmic value of the number 2?"

or, as most people would say,

"what's the log of 2"?

You're definitely going to come across this problem in your audio class. (For more information, see the section on decibels, p. 71.) Fortunately, it's easy. Type the number you want, and then press the "log10" button (Figure 1.1).

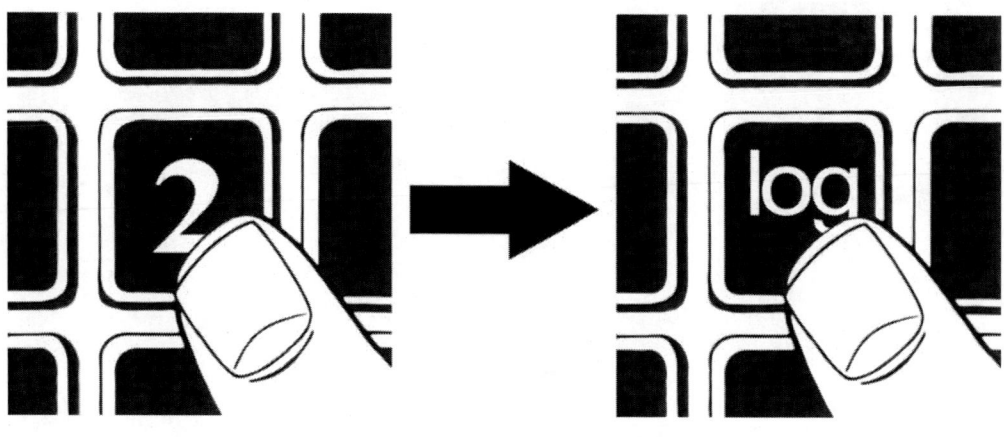

FIGURE 1.1 Calculating the log of 2

The answer is 0.301029995663981. Often, when we get a large number like this, we round the number to three significant digits. In this case, we could shorten this number to 0.301.

Clue—we found a magic number! 0.301

("Clues" are placed around the book when we touch on a concept that relates to magic numbers.)

Finding Trigonometric Values with a Calculator

Likewise, we will be looking at trigonometric functions, such as the sine function. For these functions, we will calculate the value of a point on the curve's axis, and determine where x and y intersect (Figure 1.2). We will go over more in chapter 4.

$$f(x) = \sin(x)$$

BASIC MATH REVIEW 9

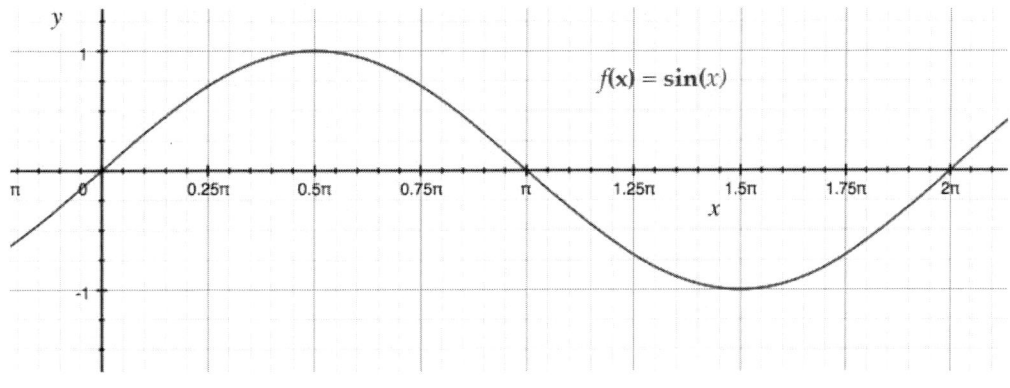

FIGURE 1.2 Graph of $y = \sin(x)$

Depending on how the x-axis is drawn, these functions require us to use either the "RAD" (radians) or "DEG" (degrees) mode on our calculator (Figure 1.3).

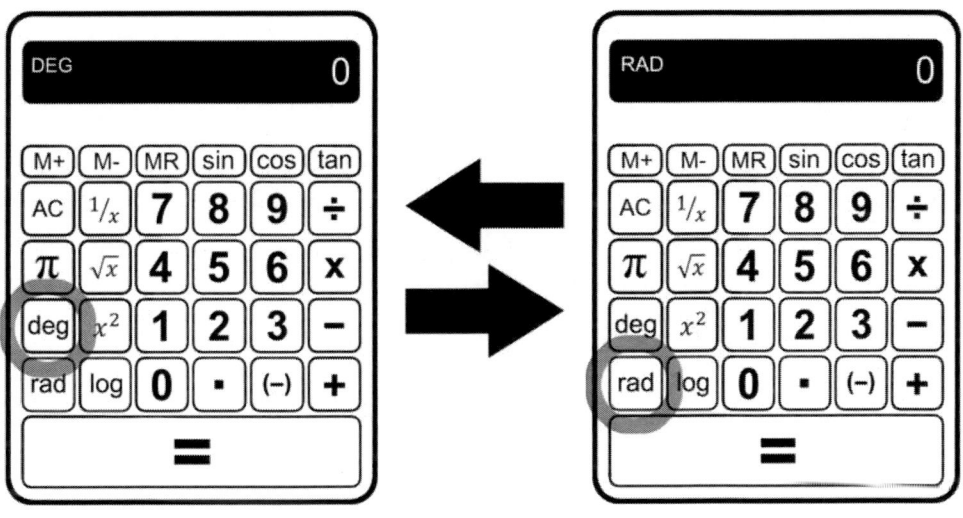

FIGURE 1.3 Switching between radians (a) and degrees (b)

You should be able to see whether your calculator is in "DEG" or "RAD" mode in your calculator's display window. If your x-axis shows degrees, your calculator should also be in the degree mode (Figure 1.4).

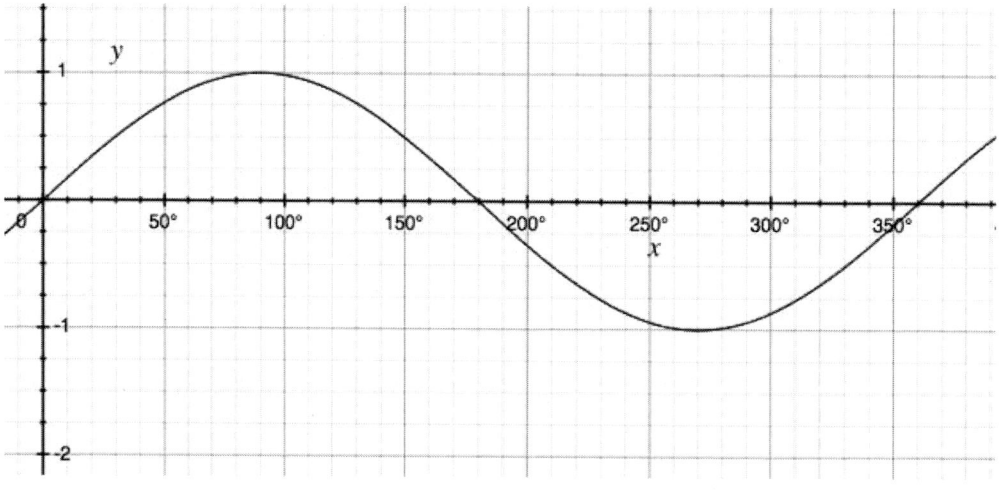

FIGURE 1.4 Graph with *x*-axis shown in degrees

If your *x*-axis shows values for π, then your calculator should be in radians mode (Figure 1.5). (We will explain more in chapters 5 and 6 when we cover trigonometry and geometry.)

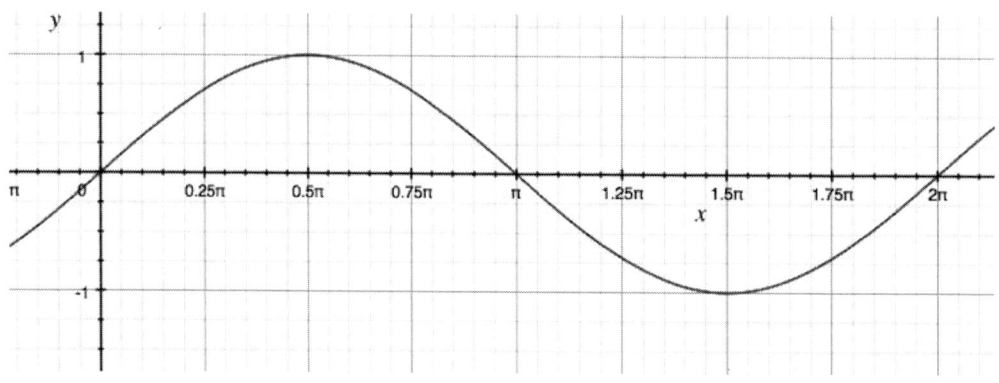

FIGURE 1.5 Graph with *x*-axis shown in radians

So, to find the value of

$$f = \sin(x)$$

at a certain value, simply enter that value, and then press the "sin" button.
In Figure 1.6, we are looking for the sine value of π:

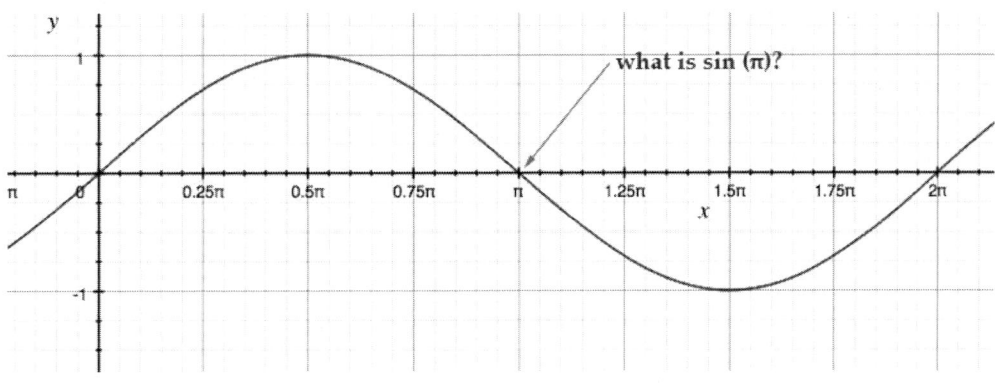

FIGURE 1.6 Sine function in radians

To find the value of $\sin \pi$, you can look on the graph or use a calculator. In Figure 1.7, where $x = \pi$, $y = 0$, so $\sin(\pi) = 0$.

12 MATH FUNDAMENTALS FOR AUDIO

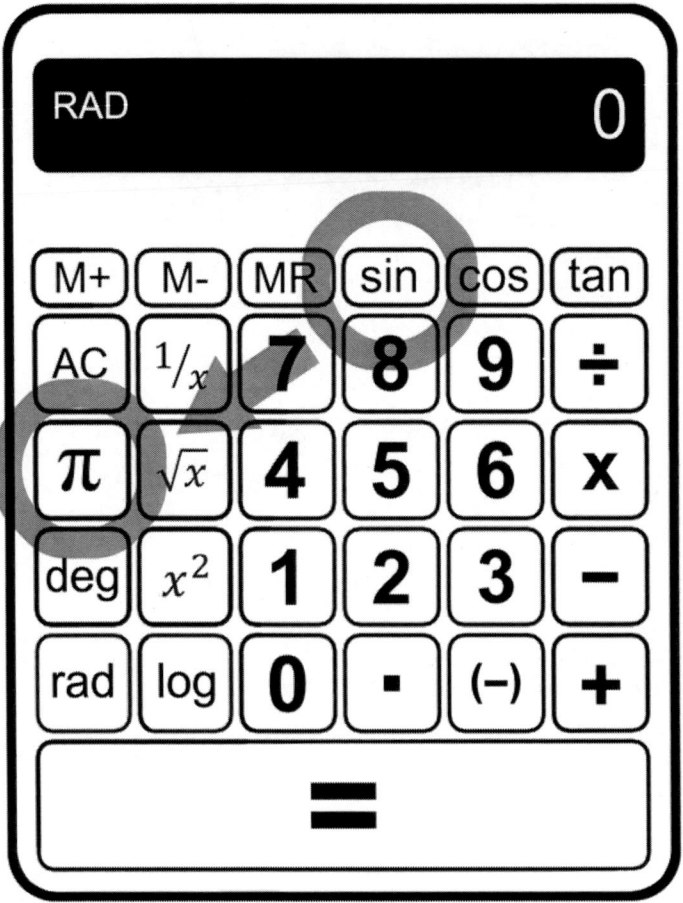

FIGURE 1.7 Sine π on a calculator

Note that the display shows "Rad" for radians.

In Figure 1.8, we are looking for the sin of 180°.

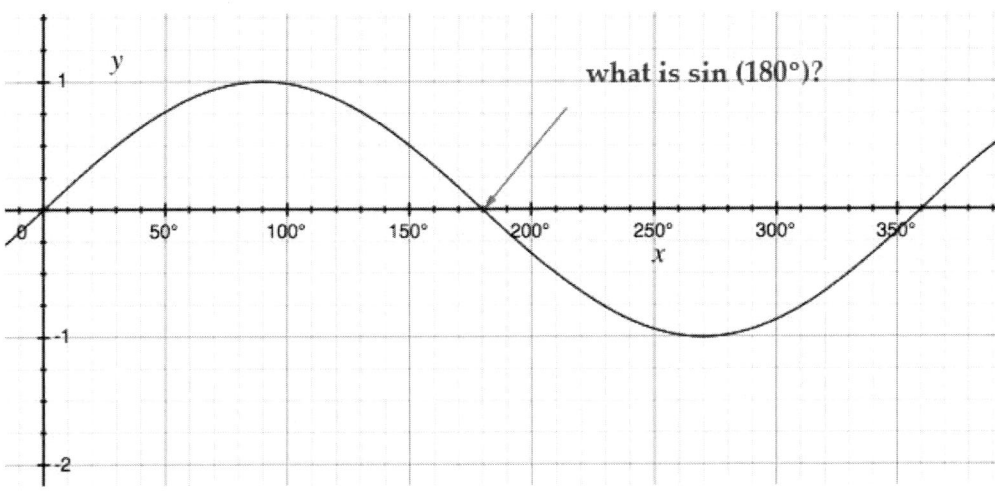

FIGURE 1.8 Sine function in degrees

To find the value of sin 180°, you can look on the graph. Where $x = 180°$, $y = 0$, so the answer again is 0. If you use a calculator, make sure that you are in degrees (DEG) mode (Figure 1.9). First, enter 180 on the calculator.

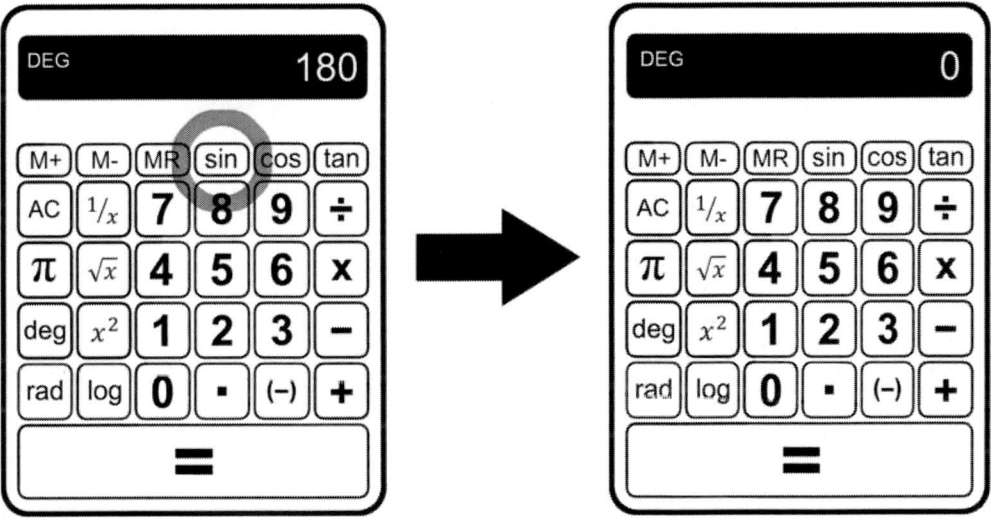

FIGURE 1.9 Sine 180° on a calculator

Notice the difference? It's important to be careful: if you enter the term "180" while in radians mode, you will get the value -0.801152635733831. This is *not* the value of $f(x) = \sin x$ at 180°. It's always helpful to draw out a graph even if you have a calculator handy, just to make sure your answers make sense (Figure 1.10).

FIGURE 1.10 When your calculator is in the wrong mode

More to Know

You can think of a radian as *the angle opposite an arc of a circle whose length is equal to the radius of the same circle (Figure 1.11).*

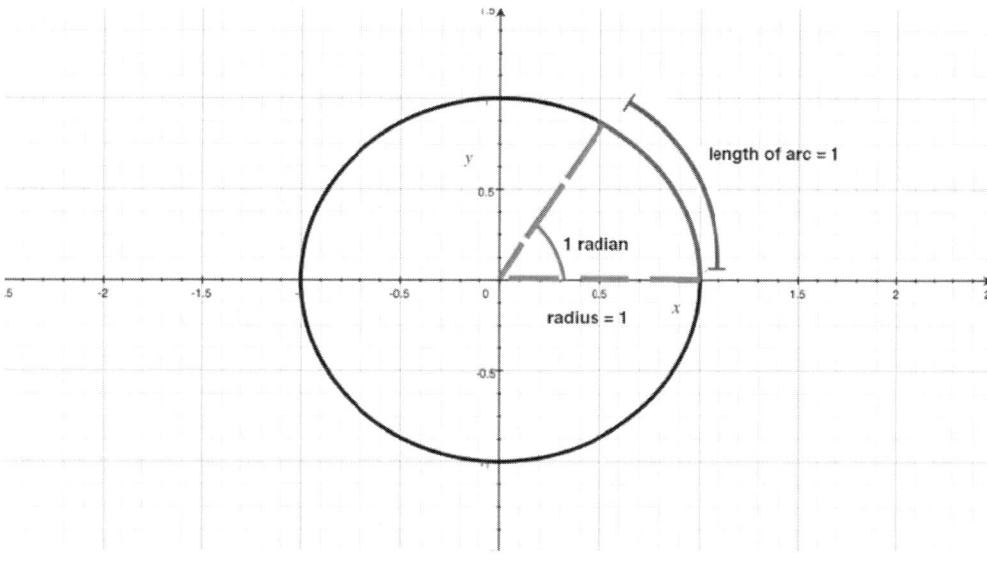

FIGURE 1.11 What one radian looks like

Another trick here is that the values on the *x*-axis may require you to do some calculation first. For example, to find the sin of 2π, you have to multiply π by 2, then hit "sin" (Figure 1.12).

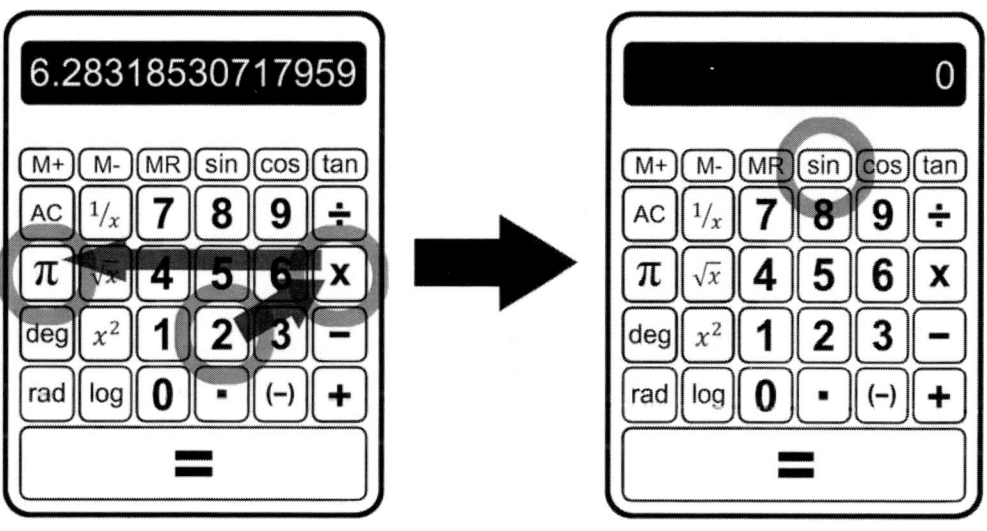

FIGURE 1.12 Calculating sin (2π)

Connecting Components

Here are some exercises you can try.

Exercise 1-1

Fill out the table below with the values for *x* using the appropriate column. If *x* is a value of π, which column do you use to write the answer? If *x* is given in degrees, in which column would you write the answer?

X	DEG	RAD
π		
$\pi/2$		
270°		
45°		
$\pi/4$		
$(3\pi)/2$		

See solutions at end of book.

Exercise 1-2

Using a calculator, find values for the following:

a) $\dfrac{\pi}{2} =$

b) $\dfrac{3\pi}{2} =$

c) $\dfrac{\pi}{4} =$

THE INVERSE FUNCTION AND INVERSE RELATIONSHIPS

You may hear that two things are "inversely proportional" to one another. Look at the following equation:

$$y = \frac{1}{x}$$

If x is a very large number, then y is a very small number. For example, if x is 1,000 then y is 0.001, or "one thousandth." But if x is a very small number, then y is big. If x is 0.001, then y is 1,000—a very large number. As x gets smaller, y gets larger. As x gets larger, y gets smaller. This is an inverse relationship.

Consider the "Q" (quality factor) measurement on a parametric equalizer (Figure 1.13).

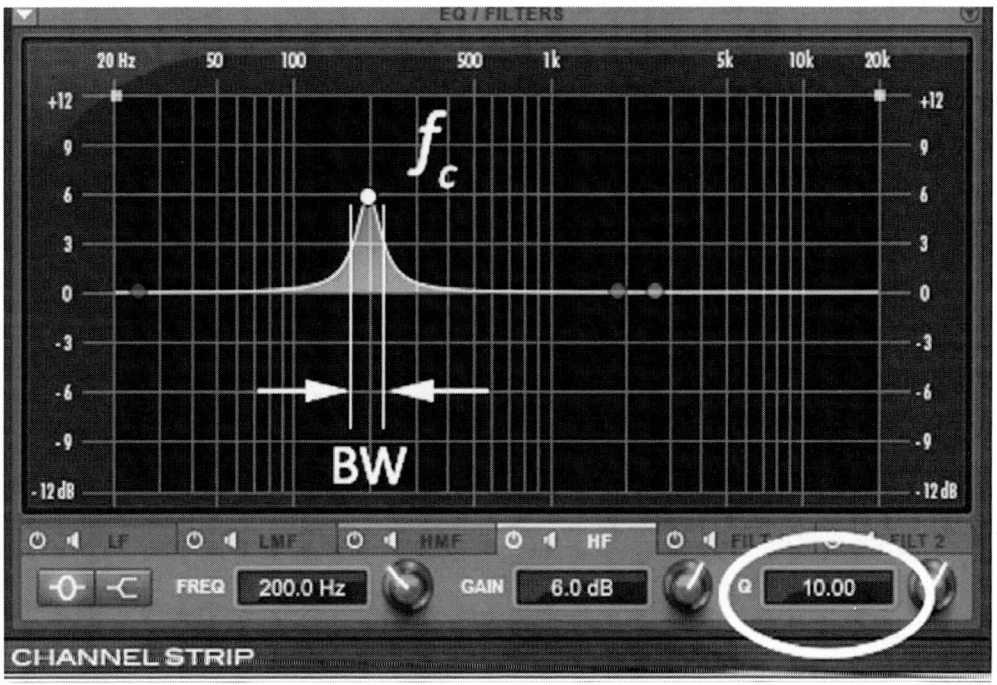

FIGURE 1.13 6 dB boost at 200 Hz, $Q = 10$

Similarly, the equation that describes Q and bandwidth is given as:

$$Q = \frac{f_c}{BW}$$

The bandwidth is measured at 3 dB below the center frequency (f_c = 200Hz). (Note: if the gain is 3 dB or less this does not apply.) If the bandwidth is wide, then the Q is small (a wide curve); likewise, a small bandwidth yields a high Q (a narrow curve). For more on Q and bandwidth, see chapter 5, "Audio and Geometry."

THE INVERSE FUNCTION AND SIMPLE CIRCUITS

The inverse function is also useful when calculating resistors in parallel. The memory function will add values together "in the background" and then recall them for you. Consider this figure:

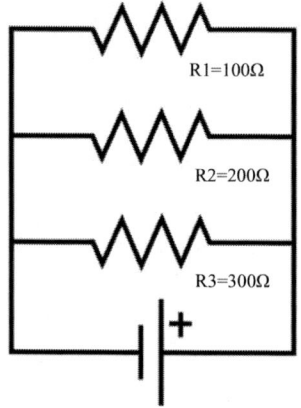

FIGURE 1.14 Three resistors in parallel

The way to find the total resistance is to use the equation:

$$R_T = \frac{1}{\frac{1}{R_1} + \frac{1}{R_2} + \cdots + \frac{1}{R_n}}$$

R_T is the total resistance. R_1 is the value of the first resistor, R_2 is the value of the second, and so on. In the case of this equation, it's

$$R_T = \frac{1}{\frac{1}{100\Omega} + \frac{1}{200\Omega} + \frac{1}{300\Omega}}$$

(Note: resistance is measured in ohms, denoted by the Greek letter Ω.)

In order to do that on a calculator, you can use the inverse key and memory keys. Use the "M+" key to add each value to the memory. First, find the inverse of 100Ω (Figure 1.15).

$$\frac{1}{100\Omega} = ?$$

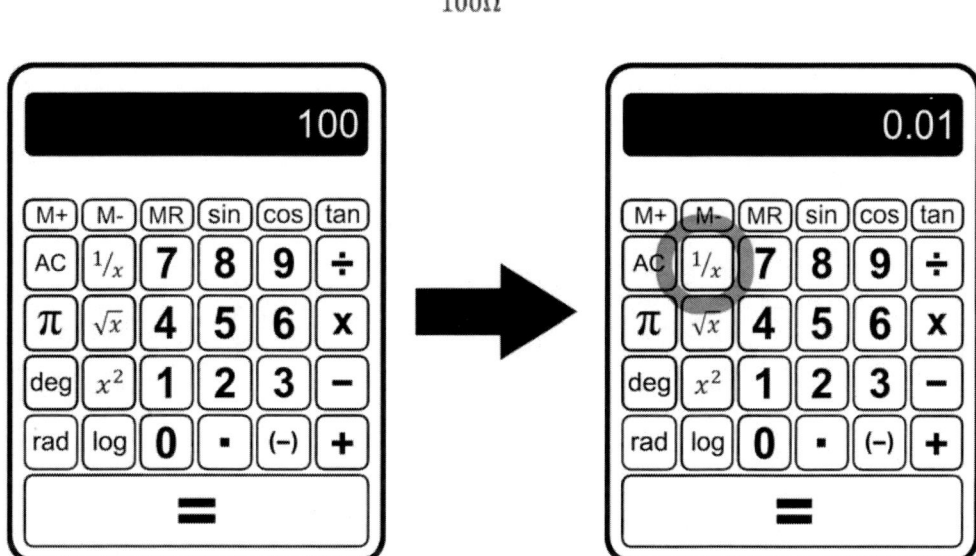

FIGURE 1.15 1/100 = 0.01

$$\frac{1}{100\Omega} = .01$$

then press the "M+" button (Figure 1.16).

20   MATH FUNDAMENTALS FOR AUDIO

FIGURE 1.16   Press "M+"

Before you perform the next calculation, you can zero out the display by hitting "AC" (All Clear) (Figure 1.17).

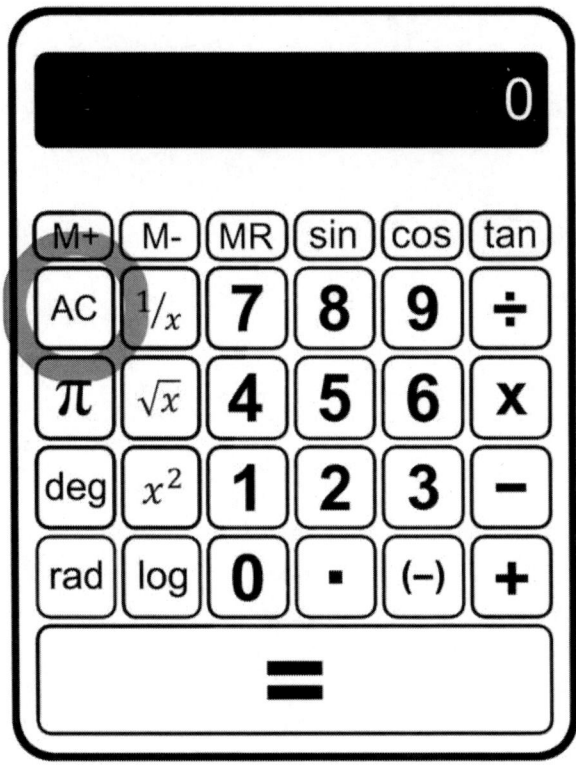

FIGURE 1.17   Press "AC," display reads "0"

If you want to be sure the number is still in the calculator's memory, hit the "MR" (Memory Recall) button and you will see ".01" reappear! Be sure to clear it before continuing by hitting "AC."

Next, find the inverse of 200Ω (Figure 1.18).

$$\frac{1}{200\Omega} = ?$$

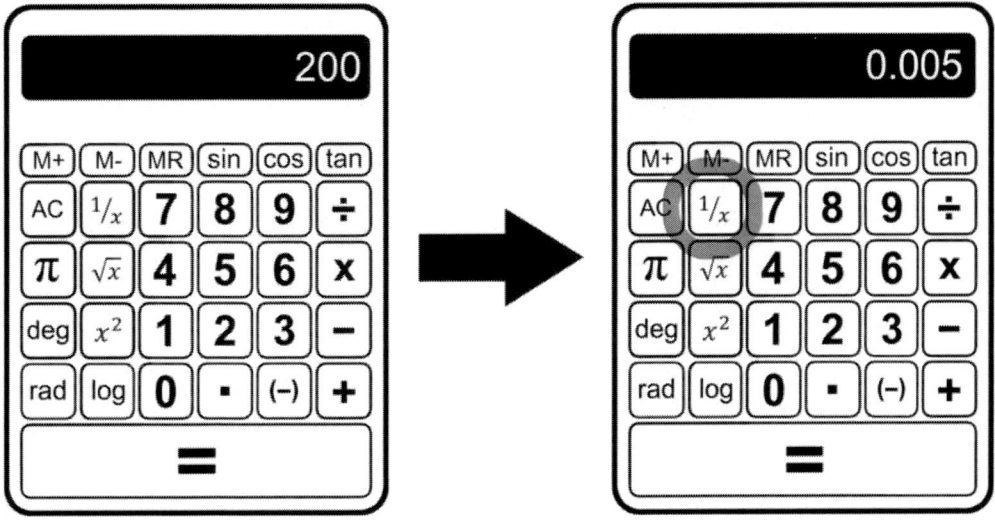

FIGURE 1.18 1/200 = 0.005

$$\frac{1}{200\Omega} = .005$$

then press the "M+" button (Figure 1.19).

FIGURE 1.19 Press "M+"

Finally, find the inverse of 300Ω (Figure 1.20),

$$\frac{1}{300\Omega} = ?$$

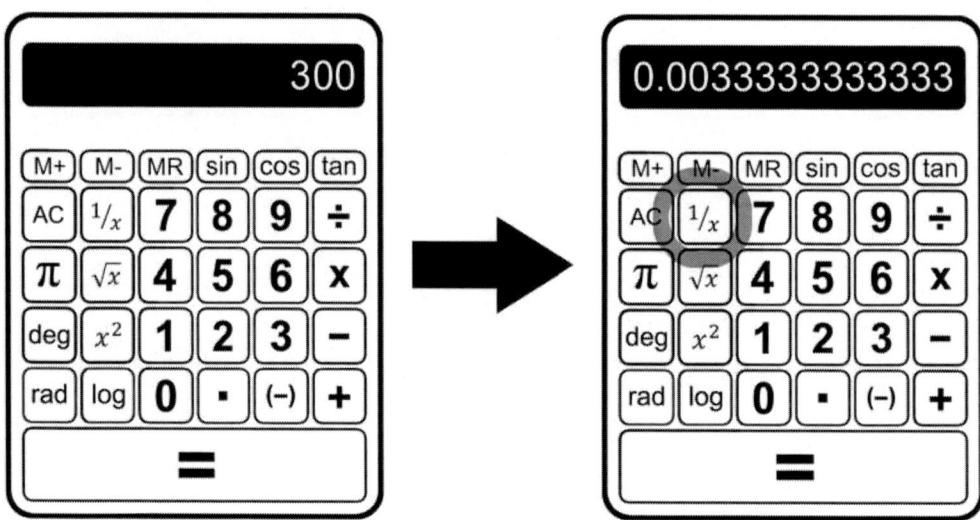

FIGURE 1.20 1/300 = 0.003

$$\frac{1}{300\Omega} = 0.00333333333333$$

then press the "M+" button (Figure 1.21).

FIGURE 1.21 Press "M+"

Once you have entered all the resistor values, press the "AC" button to zero out the display (Figure 1.22).

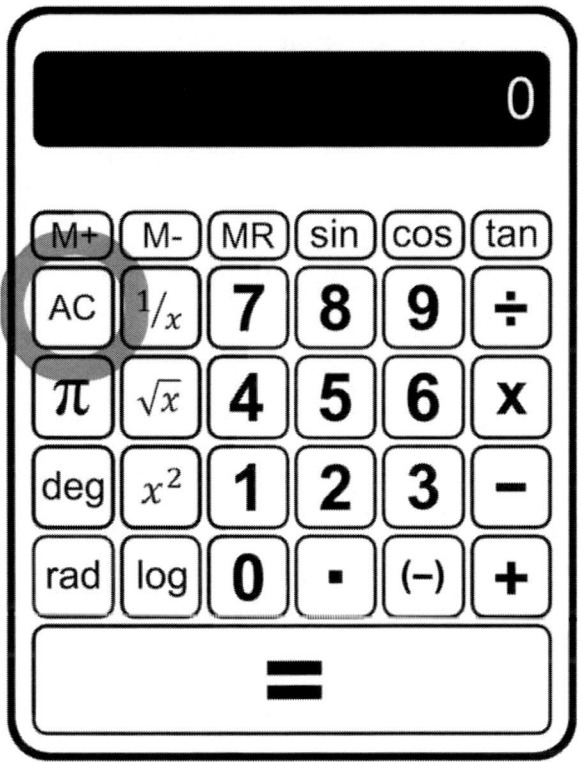

FIGURE 1.22 Press "AC," display reads "0"

During this process you have been adding numbers to the calculator's memory. By hitting the "MR" button and you will see all of your values summed together (Figure 1.23).

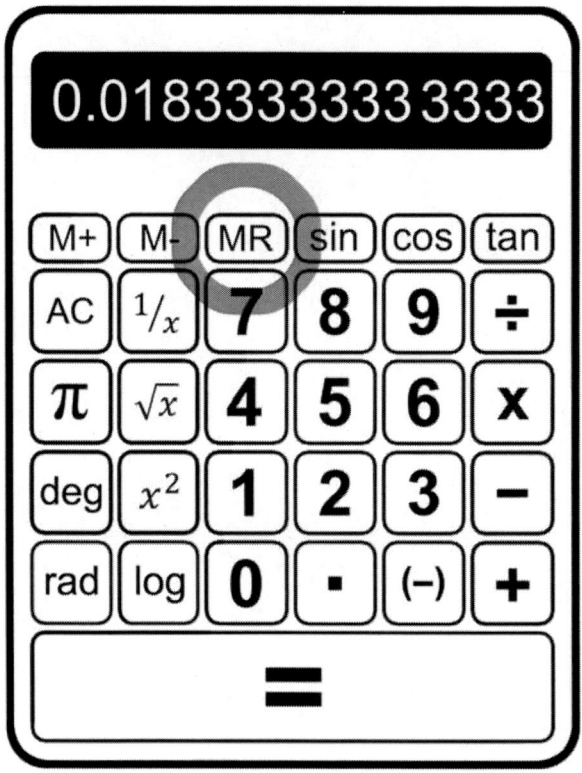

FIGURE 1.23 Sum of values held in memory

$$\frac{1}{100\Omega} + \frac{1}{200\Omega} + \frac{1}{300\Omega} = 0.0183\overline{3} \ \Omega$$

Let's just use three significant digits: 0.018Ω.

But remember, *we have only solved part of the original problem.* Here's the full equation again:

$$R_T = \frac{1}{\frac{1}{R_1} + \frac{1}{R_2} + \frac{1}{R_3}}$$

Since we just worked out the bottom part of the equation (the denominator), we can plug it in.

$$R_T = \frac{1}{0.018} \Omega$$

Now, with 0.1833333 showing in the display, press the "1/x" button again to get the answer for R_T (Figure 1.24).

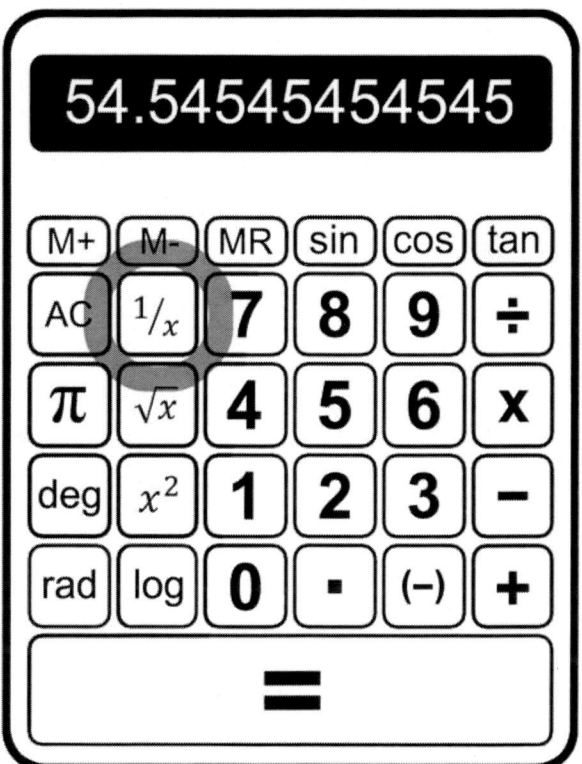

FIGURE 1.24 Final answer: the inverse of 0.018

$$\frac{1}{0.018} = 54.545 \Omega$$

The answer is a repeating decimal, 54.5454.

More to Know

Using a spreadsheet is an easy way to plug in numbers to solve equations like this.

Resistor Values	A	B	Inverse resistor values C	D	formula in column D:
	R1	100	"1/R1"	0.01	=1/B1
	R2	200	"1/R2"	0.005	=1/B2
	R3	300	"1/R3"	0.003333333	=1/B3
			subtotal	0.018333333	=sum(D2:D4)
			RT= 1/subtotal	54.54545455	=1/D5

TABLE 1.1 A spreadsheet used to calculate resistor values

Connecting Components

Here are some problems to try:

Exercise 1-3

Given five resistors in parallel all with a value of 10 Ω, what is the total resistance? Hint: Start with this equation:

$$R_T = \frac{1}{\frac{1}{R_1}+\frac{1}{R_2}+\frac{1}{R_3}+\frac{1}{R_4}+\frac{1}{R_5}}$$

Exercise 1-4

Solve the following equation to find R_T in a circuit with two branches of resistance where R_1 and R_2 are in series, both of which are in parallel with R_3. $R_1 = 5\Omega$, $R_2 = 10\Omega$, and $R_3 = 10\Omega$. Hint: Start with this equation:

$$\frac{1}{\frac{1}{R_1 + R_2} + \frac{1}{R_3}}$$

See the solutions at end of book.

CALCULATING DELAY TIMES USING PRO TOOLS

If you know the distance and time, you can find the speed (rate) of sound.

$$d = rt$$

distance = rate × time

which can also be written as

$$r = \frac{d}{t}$$

This means that if you know the distance between two microphones and can measure the time it takes to travel from one mic placed at the source and a second mic placed further away. Then, you can compare the waveforms in your favorite software (Figure 1.25).

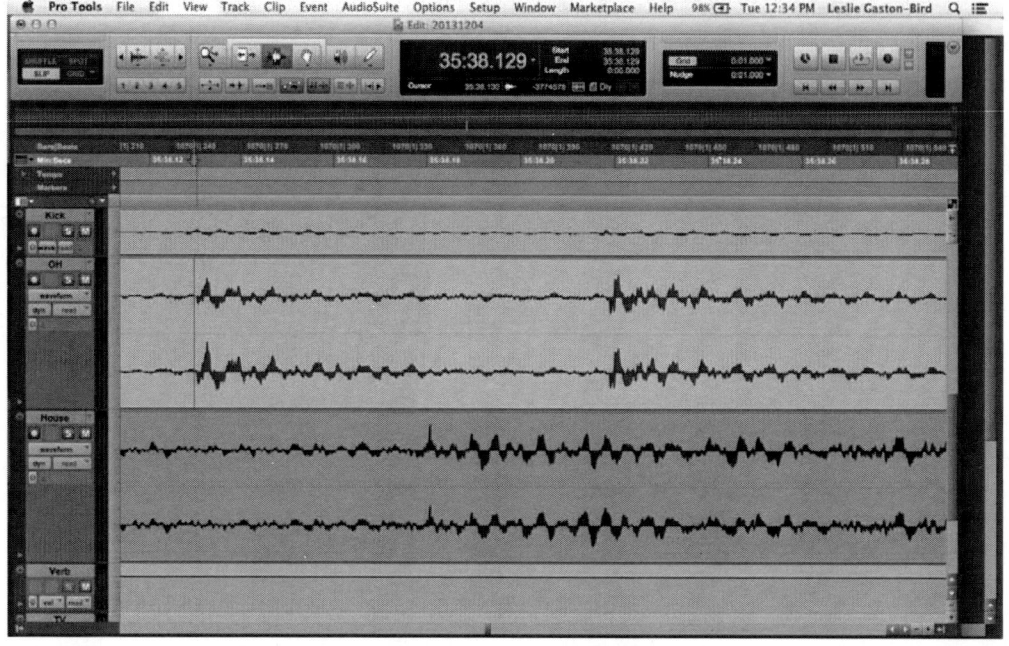

FIGURE 1.25 Pro Tools screen shot showing delay between stage mics (upper tracks) and house mics (lower tracks)

In this session you can see the signal from the "OH" (overhead) mics in the upper stereo track, and the same signal reaching the house mics ("House") slightly later. You can measure the time between those two signals and determine the delay (Figure 1.26).

BASIC MATH REVIEW

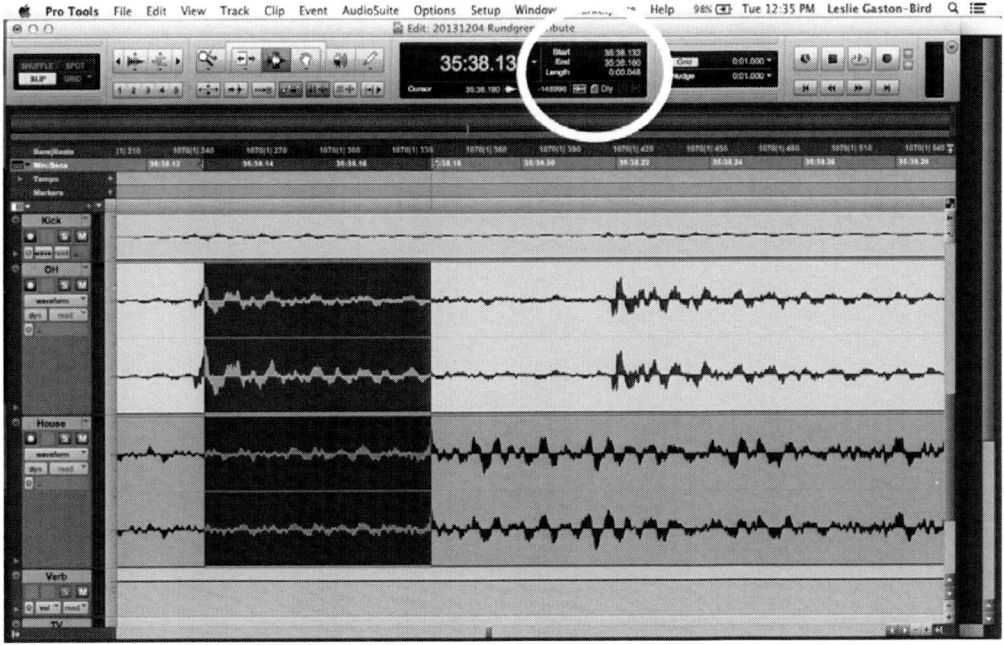

FIGURE 1.26 Vintage Pro Tools with time selected

The time it takes for the signal on the OH track to reach the house mics is 0.048 seconds, or 48 milliseconds (.001 seconds = 1 millisecond; see metric prefixes in appendix A).

 **More to Know**

Knowing that it takes 48 ms for the signal from the overheads to reach the house mics, you can now approximate the number of feet between them using the equation $d = rt$!

If you have two identical tracks, try moving them in time so one starts 48 ms later than the other. Listen with the tracks panned hard left and right. Then listen in mono. Repeat the same steps but with the tracks aligned. What are your observations?

A WORD ON LATENCY

These days, software like Pro Tools has the ability to do the math needed to compensate for the delay caused by plug-ins. But it's always nice to know what kind of math is happening inside your computer, and here's one example.

How many milliseconds of delay is caused by a plug-in that shows a 4,096 sample latency (based on a sampling frequency of 48 kHz)?

We found a clue

- The answer will be milliseconds. So, do we use the equation $d = rt$? Or something else?
- The problem has two numbers to work with: 4,096 samples and 48 kHz. The two numbers have different units, so we will have to do a conversion.

It's probably easiest to visualize this on a Pro Tools screen (Figure 1.27).

BASIC MATH REVIEW   31

FIGURE 1.27   Pro Tools screen showing delay caused by plug-in

There is a "pitch shift" plug-in on track two. That means that while the computer is busy performing the math to play back the sound, track one is already playing, and is therefore *ahead in time* by 4,096 samples. You can see the amount of delay created in the I/O window (circled in Figure 1.27). We can visualize this in a different way. Figure 1.28 shows a track delayed 4,096 samples.

FIGURE 1.28 The same track showing audio shifted 4,096 samples to the right

It would be nice to somehow "stop" (or delay) track one for the 4,096 samples it takes for track two to get processed. This way, the tracks would play back in sync. There is an easy way to do this: you can put a "time adjuster" plug-in on track one and set it to 4,096 samples.

But how long is 4,096 samples? We might need to know how these adjustments are going to interact with the other tracks in the recording. In Figure 1.28, you can see the time circled. It takes 0.085 seconds from the start of the audio until track 2 begins playing.

We can also figure this out mathematically. Because we know the sample rate of our system (48 kHz), we can determine the time required for one sample. (You can read about a similar problem when we talk about cycles per second, seconds per cycle, and hummingbird wings in the section "Cross multiplication," p. 39–41.) Forty-eight thousand samples are taken every second.

$$F_s = 48,000$$

Or, it takes one forty-eight thousandth of a second for one sample to be taken.

$$t_{1\ sample} = \frac{1}{F_s}$$

$$t_{1\ sample} = \frac{1}{48{,}000}\ seconds$$

In the case where 4,096 samples of latency are introduced, it becomes a multiplication problem: If we use t_n to denote the time for one sample, F_s for the sample rate (sample frequency), and let the number of samples (n) be equal to 1:

$$t_n = \frac{1}{F_s} \cdot n$$

$$t_1 = \frac{1}{48{,}000} \cdot 1$$

$$t_1 = 0.00002083333333$$

or about .021 ms. Then for 4,096 samples, $n = 4{,}096$:

$$t_{4096} = \frac{1}{48{,}000} \cdot 4{,}096$$

$$t_{4096} = \frac{4{,}096}{48{,}000}$$

$$t_{4096} = 0.0853\overline{3}$$

or about 85.3 ms—the same value that is shown in the Pro Tools time window. That's quite a long delay!

More to Know

If you do not have automatic delay compensation in your software, you will discover that mixing acoustic instruments (drums, acoustic guitar, etc.) is like herding cats. Every time you put in a plug-in, you are delaying the audio on that track. This is not *good* for two reasons:

1. Delay affects the **phase** of an audio signal, and combining similar signals with differing phases can result in comb filtering, and

2. The **precedence effect** (or "law of the first arriving wavefront") describes a phenomenon where, given two identical sounds, human beings use the first sound they hear to localize the sound.

So if you have two instruments with identical content (for example, a guitar amplifier with two mics, one in front and one on the side) and have both sounds panned left and right, the sound will appear to come from the center. However, if you put a plug-in (such as a compressor or pitch shift) on the left channel, the latency will cause the image to move to the right—because the left channel will be heard *after the right channel*. If you keep adding and taking away plug-ins while you mix, you might find yourself adjusting the pan pot, too!

This also impacts the sound when the audio is panned center. You will hear phase shifting causing undesirable effects. It may make your sound duller; an extreme example will produce the "vacuum hose" effect.

Let's look at this sample problem:

How many milliseconds is represented by 500 samples of delay?

$$t_n = \frac{1}{F_s} \cdot n$$

$$t_{500} = \frac{1}{48000} \cdot 500$$

$$t_{500} = \frac{500}{48000}$$

$$t_{500} = 0.0104$$

or about 10.4 milliseconds.

WORKING WITH DATA RATES

"Data rate" refers to the amount of data being played back or otherwise transferred within a certain period of time. For example, a DVD-Video disc can play back roughly only 10 megabits of data per second (10 Mbits/s)—and most of that is saved for the video data. A Blu-ray disc can handle more than 30 Mbit/s. Let's have a look at how each medium can cope with audio with this example problem:

What is the data rate for two channels of audio recorded at 48 kHz and 24 bits per sample?

For this problem, you have two channels of audio, each comprised of 48,000 samples per second. Each sample is represented by one 24-bit number. You would multiply the number of channels by the number of samples per second to get the answer.

$$data\ rate = \#\ channels \times sample\ rate \times bits$$

$$data\ rate = 2 \cdot 48,000 \frac{samples}{second} \cdot 24\ bits$$

$$data\ rate = 96,000 \frac{samples}{second} \cdot 24\ bits$$

$$data\ rate = \frac{2,304,000\ bits}{second}$$

$$data\ rate = 2.305\ megabits/second$$

This implies that if you want to listen to full-fidelity, stereo audio on a DVD-Video disc, a Blu-ray disc, or even with a high-speed data connection, it should be possible (as long as there is no video data to compete with for space!). Will the same hold true for 5.1 audio?

Exercise 1-5

What is the data rate for 5.1 channels of audio recorded at 48 kHz and 24 bits?

This is a trick question, because 5.1 channels are really 5.005 channels. Of course you are asking, "How was I supposed to know that?" Well, you wouldn't know unless you had studied surround sound and knew that the LFE (Low Frequency Effects or Low Frequency Extension) channel has a smaller bandwidth than the other channels.

The original question, now reworded with 5.005 instead of 5.1, is:

What is the data rate for 5.005 channels of audio recorded at 48 kHz and 24 bits?

$$data\ rate = \#\ channels \times sample\ rate \times bits$$

$$data\ rate = 5.005 \times 48,000 \frac{samples}{second} \times 24\ bits$$

See the solution at end of book.

More to Know

In a 5.1 system, the left, center, right, left surround, and right surround channels reproduce frequencies from 20 to 20,000 Hz, but the LFE channel reproduces sounds from only 20 to 120 Hz. In most cases, the audio data needs to be compressed in order to fit on a disc with video. The bandwidth for the full-range channels is 19,980 (20,000 - 20) Hz. The bandwidth of the LFE is 100 (120 - 20) Hz. Here is the ratio of LFE to a full range channel:

$$\frac{100}{19,980} = .005$$

So it's really more accurate to call a 5.1 system a "5.005" system!

Exercise 1-6

Given that the data rate of a DVD-Video disc is 10 Mbits/s, can it accommodate 5.005 channels of audio? Use the answer from Exercise 1-5 for your answer. See the solution at the end of book.

TWO
Audio and Algebra

"ALPHABET SOUP" OF AUDIO: SYMBOLS AND TERMS

In chapter 1 we reviewed how to solve for a variable. But there's more to it than just *a*, *b*, and *c*. Table 2.1 lists some of the commonly used variables found in many audio textbooks. Some of these variables come with an additional term called "subscript notation"—for example, X_C, a term used for *capacitive reactance*. The X stands for reactance, and the c stands for capacitance. You don't multiply X by c in this case; you treat the entire term as one variable.

F	Frequency
f_{max}	maximum frequency
f_{min}	minimum frequency
f_c	Center frequency
c	Speed of sound
dB	Decibel
dBm	Decibels (with a reference of 1 milliwatt)
dB SPL	Decibels of "sound pressure level"
θ	Lower case theta, a Greek character representing degree or phase angle (with a reference of 20 micropascals)
ω	Lower case omega, a Greek character representing frequency in radians per second
X_L	Inductive Reactance
X_C	Capacitive Reactance
Z	Impedance

TABLE 2.1 Examples of variables

There are several other terms besides those in Table 2.1, of course. The point here is that you can set up equations with these terms just as you do with *a, b,* or *c.* For example, if you see an equation like

$$A = \frac{I_a}{I_r}$$

then your textbook should provide an explanation of what each letter means. In this case, *A* is an "absorption coefficient," I_a is the amount of sound energy absorbed, and I_r is the amount of sound energy reflected.

More to Know

You can think of the subscript letters act as "helpers": The "a" stands for "absorbed" and the "r" stands for "reflected."

In order to solve this equation, you need to be provided with values for at least two of the three variables *A*, I_a, or I_r before you can solve the problem. In some cases, however, you have to find the values yourself or be familiar with some common "reference" values. For example, here is the equation for determining sound pressure level:

$$L_p = 20 \log \frac{p_{rms}}{p_{ref}} \, dB$$

L_p represents the "Level of pressure." P_{rms} is a root-mean-squared (rms) measurement of pressure, and p_{ref} is the basis for the measurement—in this case, the smallest sound humans can detect. The answer will be given in decibels (dB). In order to solve the equation, you might be expected to know a value for p_{ref}. In this case, the value is 20 micro Pascals (20μPa).

More to Know

The previous equation is given to show the parts of a typical equation. In order to solve, you need a value for p_{rms}. This should be given in Pascals as well.

CROSS MULTIPLICATION

A lot of what we will be doing in the book involves "cross-multiplying." Here's an equation you might have seen in algebra class:

$$a = bc$$

As an example, this could mean

$$12 = 2 \cdot c$$

where $a = 12$ and $b = 2$, or

$$12 = b \cdot 6$$

where $a = 12$ and $c = 6$, or

$$a = 2 \cdot 6.$$

where $b = 2$ and $c = 6$.

In each example, we multiply by the reciprocal to get the unknown term on one side of the equation.

In the following example, we are solving for c, so to get the two on the correct side of the equation, we multiply both sides by the reciprocal of 2 (which is 1/2):

$$12 = 2 \cdot c$$

$$\frac{1}{2} \cdot 12 = \cancel{2} \cdot \frac{1}{\cancel{2}} \cdot c$$

$$6 = c$$

 **Morc to Know**

Consider of a pair of scales. Each side of the "equals" sign balances the equation.

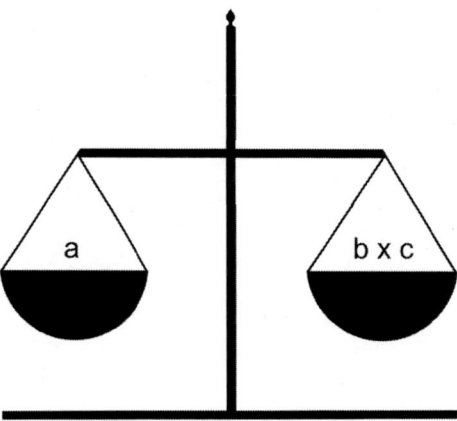

FIGURE 2.1 A scale showing two sides of a balanced equation

If you change one side of the equation, the scales are no longer balanced.

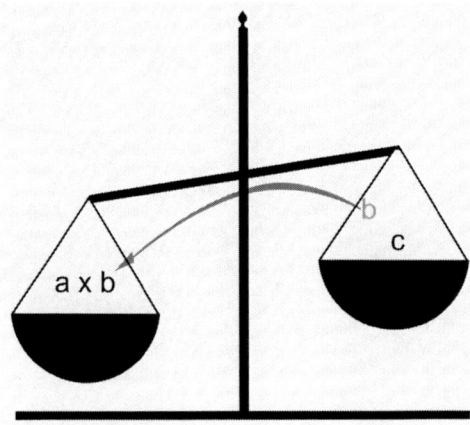

FIGURE 2.2 The scale is unbalanced when a term is moved

You must add the same term to both sides of the equation to balance it again.

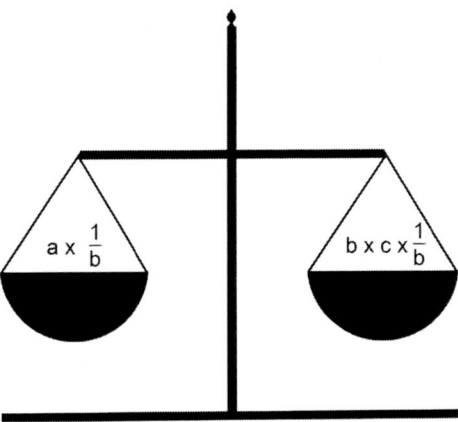

FIGURE 2.3 The scale is balanced again when "like" terms are used on both sides

DISTANCE, RATE, TIME, WAVELENGTH, AND FREQUENCY

You have no doubt run into this problem as an audio student: you have to convert between feet and meters (also spelled "metres"). Depending on the textbook, you've learned that sound travels either 1130 feet per second or 343 meters per second. But those two distances are not the same. Go to your favorite conversion calculator or "app" and investigate:

1130 feet per second = 344.424 meters per second (not 343!)

and

343 meters per second = 1125.33 feet per second (not 1130!)

It's very important to come to an agreement about the reference points you are using with your audio team (classmates, professor, or coworkers).

 **More to Know**

The Mars Orbiter completely missed its target because one group of scientists was using meters and the other group was using feet! (Source: http://mars.nasa.gov/msp98/news/mco990930.html)

The speed of sound can also vary with temperature and altitude. The best way to determine the speed of sound—if you are in a situation where that knowledge is critical—is to calculate it. This book is a meant to be companion guide to your audio textbook, so you have likely already found equation 2-4, which reads, "The speed of sound (c) is equal to the wavelength (λ) times the frequency (f)." λ is the Greek letter lambda (pronounced LAM-da).

$$c = \lambda f$$

But if you are trying to calculate the speed of sound, you might recall another formula, $d = rt$, which we will discuss in the next section.

CALCULATING WAVELENGTHS AND FREQUENCIES

George is driving a European car to Milwaukee, which is 316,800 feet away. His speedometer reads only kilometers per hour. How fast does he need to go (in km/h) to arrive in Milwaukee in 60 minutes?

Why are we talking about cars? And don't European cars have both kilometer and mile measurements on the speedometer? Of course, but it's important with any mathematical concept to begin on familiar ground. When concepts become complex, it's sometimes helpful to use an example you can grasp more easily—driving a car, for example. If you are driving 60 miles per hour and your destination is 60 miles away, how long will it take you to arrive? One hour, of course.

Now what fool would give you driving directions in feet? (Hopefully you don't know anyone this mean-spirited.) But in reality, we are always having to convert between units. So, this exercise is not as silly as it may seem. We can find the answer by converting feet to kilometers, using the equation

$$d = rt$$

where d = distance, r = rate, and t = time.

Let's start by starting by solving for r, because we are interested in how fast George needs to drive:

$$r = \frac{d}{t}$$

Then we need to be sure get our answer in kilometers per hour.

$$r = \frac{316{,}800 \; feet}{60 \; minutes}$$

We can hopefully convert minutes to hours easily: 60 minutes equals 1 hour.

$$r = \frac{316{,}800 \; feet}{1 \; hour}$$

Converting from feet to meters, however, is not so easy. We can go to Google and ask, "what is 316,800 feet in kilometers", which will quickly return the number 96.56064. Or, if we are given 1 foot = 0.0003048 kilometers:

$$1 \; foot = 0.0003048 \; km$$

Then we just need to "balance our scales" by multiplying both sides by 316,800:

$$1 \; foot \times 316{,}800 = 0.0003048 \; km \times 316{,}800$$

$$316{,}800 \; feet = 96.56064 \; km$$

Now you'll learn how driving a European car to Milwaukee can help with studying audio theory. Distance, rate, and time are related to three easily recognized acoustic parameters: **Wavelength**, **frequency**, and the **speed of sound**.

Wavelength corresponds to distance. Its symbol is a lower case Greek letter "lambda":

λ = wavelength, measured in feet, meters, inches, centimeters, etc.

FIGURE 2.4 A car is used to illustrate wavelength

As seen in Figure 2.4, the wavelength of this sine wave is shown by the distance from one point of the wave to the next repeating point on the wave, usually measured from one peak or trough to the next. If you want to stick with the car analogy, it's the distance you would "drive" from one point to the next similar point.

Frequency corresponds to time—more precisely, to the inverse of time. Time can be measured in seconds, but frequency (f) describes *the number of vibrations (cycles) that happen in one second.* One Hertz (Hz) equals one cycle per second. Therefore, the phrase "there are a hundred cycles per second" (100 Hz) is the same as the phrase, "every 1/100th of a second there is one cycle."

 **More to Know**

What's easier to say: "How long does it take a hummingbird to beat its wings, 500 times?" or "How many times per second can a hummingbird beat its wings"? One is expressed as time (how long it takes) and one is expressed as frequency (how many times per second).

In other words, here is an expression for frequency

$$f = \frac{100 \; cycles}{1 \; second}$$

and one for time (T, or the "period" of the wave):

$$T = \frac{1 \; cycle}{100th \; of \; a \; second}$$

The relationship between time and frequency is

$$T = \frac{1}{f}$$

and

$$f = \frac{1}{T}$$

This is what we mean by "the inverse of time." (Likewise, time is the inverse of frequency.) When we plug those terms into our equation, it looks like this:

$$T = \frac{1}{f}$$

Since time = 1 second / 100 vibrations, and frequency = 100 cycles/second, then

$$\frac{1\ second}{100\ vibrations} = \frac{1}{\frac{100\ cycles}{1\ second}}$$

The "seconds" term on the right hand side of the equation moves to the numerator, because dividing is the same as multiplying by the reciprocal:

$$\frac{1}{\frac{a}{b}} = \frac{b}{a}$$

and

$$1 \div \frac{a}{b} = 1 \times \frac{b}{a}$$

In our example:

$$\frac{1}{\frac{100\ cycles}{1\ second}}$$

is the same as writing

$$1 \cdot \frac{1\ second}{100\ cycles}$$

which leaves us with the balanced equation,

$$\frac{1\ second}{100\ cycles} = \frac{1\ second}{100\ cycles}$$

The **speed of sound**, written as c, corresponds to rate. But ask an audio engineer what the speed of sound is, and you probably won't get an answer in miles per hour. You'll either hear:

"The speed of sound is 1130 feet per second"

or

"The speed of sound is 343 meters per second."

Also, the speed varies depending on altitude and temperature.

 **We found a clue**

If you can remember that $d = rt$, then you can establish that $c = \lambda f$ like this.

$$d = rt$$

corresponds to

$$\lambda = c \cdot \frac{1}{f}$$

because distance (d) corresponds to λ, rate (r) corresponds to the speed of sound, and time (t) corresponds to the inverse of frequency. A neater way to write this is to get rid of the f in the denominator by multiplying both sides by its reciprocal:

$$\frac{f}{1} \cdot \lambda = \frac{c}{f} \cdot \frac{f}{1}$$

Cross out the similar terms:

$$\frac{f}{1} \cdot \lambda = \frac{c}{\cancel{f}} \cdot \frac{\cancel{f}}{1}$$

$$f \cdot \lambda = c$$

Or, as it is commonly written:

$$c = \lambda f$$

 **More to Know**

Another way to find an equivalent expression is to draw a triangle where the top is one side of the equation and the bottom is the other.

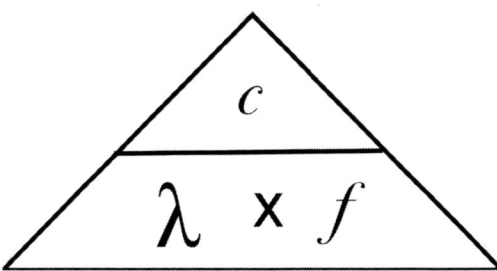

If you place your finger over the term you want, you will see how to solve the equation. In this figure, we want to find the frequency, "f". By placing your finger over the "f", the triangle shows the answer is "c over lambda"

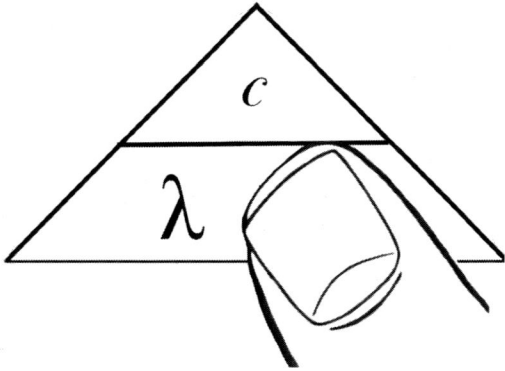

Let's do an exercise and see how this works.

Exercise 2-1

What is the length of a sound wave with a frequency of 550 Hz?

As you have read in your audio textbook, determining a wavelength (λ) is helpful when finding standing waves in a room or frequencies that might cancel between two microphones. But one thing is missing from our question: In what units should our answer be—feet or meters? Just as in our "driving to Milwaukee" question, we need to know if we're working with feet, inches, or meters.

Tip: higher frequencies usually have shorter wavelengths. But since 550 Hz is a "mid" frequency, we might want to start with feet or meters. Why not? Let's find the answer in *both* feet and meters.

First, let's start with the formula
$$c = \lambda f$$
In the last section, the speed of sound (c) was given as either 343 meters or 1130 feet per second. Let's use meters first.

   a. *Find the length of a 550 Hz wave in meters using $c = 343$ m/s.*

First we set up the equation:
$$c = \lambda f$$

$$\frac{343 \ meters}{1 \ second} = \lambda \cdot \frac{550 \ cycles}{1 \ second}$$

In order to get the lambda on one side of the equation, we multiply both sides by the reciprocal of 550 cycles / 1 second:

$$\frac{1 \ second}{550 \ cycles} \cdot \frac{343 \ meters}{1 \ second} = \lambda \cdot \frac{550 \ cycles}{1 \ second} \cdot \frac{1 \ second}{550 \ cycles}$$

$$\frac{\cancel{1 \ second}}{550 \ cycles} \cdot \frac{343 \ meters}{\cancel{1 \ second}} = \lambda$$

$$\frac{343 \ meters}{550 \ cycles} = \lambda$$

$$\frac{.624 \ meters}{cycles} = \lambda$$

Because wavelength is defined as the distance of *one* cycle, we can simply write

$$.624 \ meters = \lambda$$

   b. *Find the length of a 550 Hz wave in feet.*

$$c = \lambda f$$

$$\frac{1130 \ feet}{1 \ second} = \lambda \cdot \frac{550 \ cycles}{1 \ second}$$

$$\frac{1 \ \cancel{second}}{550 \ cycles} \cdot \frac{1130 \ feet}{1 \ \cancel{second}} = \lambda$$

$$\frac{1130 \ feet}{550 \ cycles} = \lambda$$

$$\frac{2.055 \ feet}{cycles} = \lambda$$

It is worth noting at this point that 2.055 feet is equivalent to 0.674 meters. But wait—why did we find an answer of 0.624 meters in exercise 2? Recall that 1130 feet/second is not the same as 343 meters/second (see the previous section). It is important to realize that some of the numbers that your colleagues and classmates use are only a matter of convenience, not accuracy!

$$0.624 \neq 0.674$$

So which one is correct? Well, to determine the speed of sound where you are, you could (1) determine the air temperature and use an app or online program to tell the answer, or (2) measure the distance to the point you want to measure (d) and use the time difference (t) between a microphone on stage and the microphone at the distance you measured, and then solve the equation $t = d/r$. The important thing to remember is the next time you have an exam, make sure that your professor tells you what he or she is using for c!

CALCULATING DELAY TIMES USING ALGEBRA

Suppose you are at a concert or lecture in a large hall and someone is speaking or singing on stage. If you are in the front row, it takes a short amount of time for their voice to reach you. If you are in the back of the hall, it takes longer for their voice to reach you; not only that, it might be more difficult to hear depending on the reverberation of the hall (Figure 2.2).

To compensate for this, the person on stage will probably be given a microphone. This solves one problem (at least now you can hear the voice) but creates another: there will be a delay between (a) the signal from the microphone, which reaches you almost instantaneously (assuming you are sitting right next to the loudspeaker), and (b) the acoustic signal coming from the stage.

In order to address this new delay problem, sound reinforcement engineers add a delay to the loudspeaker. If there is more than one loudspeaker (usually along the walls in an auditorium), then a different delay is applied to each loudspeaker, depending on the distance from the source.

> *Problem: What is the delay time needed for a loudspeaker 5 meters away from a source?*

The goal here is for the arrival time of the acoustic sound to at least match up with the arrival time of the audio from the loudspeaker. (In reality, the signal is delayed a bit more so that the audience can localize the performer on stage, but we will keep this example simple). Without delays, the loudspeaker would be heard before the sound gets to the listening position at A and B. The result would be an echo that could adversely affect intelligibility.

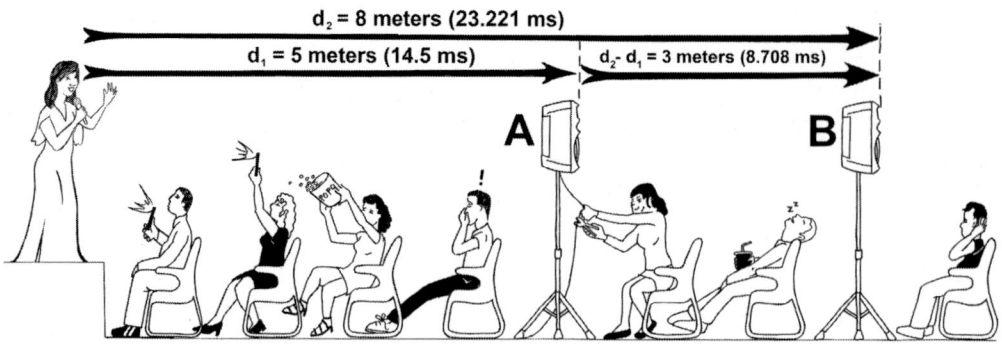

FIGURE 2.5 Two loudspeakers at different distances from the source

Based on what you have read so far, which equation do you think is better for calculating delay times? Is it

$$c = \lambda f$$

or

$$d = rt?$$

Because we are solving for time, $d = rt$ is the correct equation to use. The speed of sound is independent of frequency and wavelength. Thus, the two variables (λ and f) will not affect delay time. You are correct, however, if you thought that the value of c will be used in place of r in our equation.

$$r = c = \text{the speed of sound}$$

Just as you should be careful about what value you use for c, you should be wary of another commonly used—but slightly inaccurate—method for calculating delay times. Many audio engineers use the "1 millisecond per foot" rule when calculating delay times for loudspeakers or microphones. It is only 1 ms/foot, however, if the speed of sound is 1,000 feet per second—a condition that is true only at –43.5º Fahrenheit (–41.95º Celsius)! (See http://www.sengpielaudio.com/calculator-speedsound.htm.)

Let's assume instead that the air temperature is 72º Fahrenheit, which gives us a c of 1,130.297 feet per second. That's 344.51 meters per second. Thus, the amount of time it takes sound to reach the listener 5 meters away from the source is found this way:

$$d = rt$$

or

$$t = \frac{d}{r}$$

$$t = \frac{5m}{344.51\frac{m}{s}}$$

$$t = .014513\ seconds$$

A list of metric prefixes is provided in appendix A. There, you will see that .001 seconds is 1 millisecond, so it follows that we can write .014513 seconds as 14.513 milliseconds (or 14.513 ms). Thus, the delay required on the loudspeaker is 14.5 ms.

Now, try this:

> *Problem: What are the delay times needed to align a loudspeaker 5 meters away from a source with one 8 meters away from the same source?*

Now we are given *two* distances to work with: 5 meters and 8 meters. Again, we are going to use our favorite equation $d = rt$, but how? If you're not sure where to start, why not solve what you can and make a few discoveries? So let's dive right in and solve $d = rt$ for all of the distances involved.

More to Know

Just as we used a triangle as a "shortcut" to figure out how to create an equivalent expression for $c = \lambda f$, we can do the same for $d = rt$:

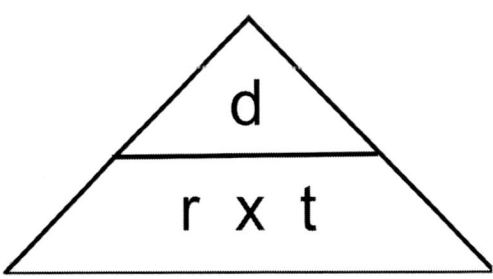

FIGURE 2.6 A triangle showing the equation $d = rt$

52 MATH FUNDAMENTALS FOR AUDIO

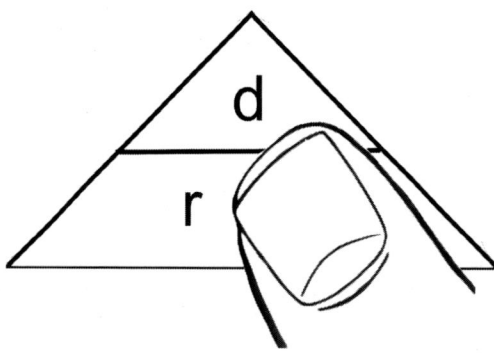

FIGURE 2.7 Cover the desired term with your finger to see the equation

To solve for t, divide distance by rate:

$$t = \frac{d}{r}$$

In our work above on the delay time needed for a loudspeaker 5 meters away from a source (p. 51), the answer was 14.513 ms. The amount of time it takes sound to reach the listener 8 meters away is

$$d = rt$$

$$t = \frac{8m}{344.51\frac{m}{s}}$$

$$t = .023221 \: seconds$$

or 23.221 ms. These are the delay times. It will take 14.513 ms for sound from the stage to reach the loudspeaker A, and 23.221 ms for sound to reach loudspeaker B.

Another way to solve this problem would have been to include all of the variables in one equation, using subscript notation, and determine the *difference* in time between the two loudspeakers. The delay times could be noted as t_1 and t_2. To solve the equation, we could use

$$t_{difference} = t_2 - t_1$$

$$8.708 \: ms = 23.221 \: ms - 14.513 \: ms$$

Here's another approach to the problem. We can find another equation to use so that we only need the variables we know. Because $t = d/r$:

$$t_{delay} = t_2 - t_1$$

$$t_{delay} = \frac{d_2}{r} - \frac{d_1}{r}$$

When subtracting with a common denominator, the equation becomes:
$$t_{delay} = \frac{d_2 - d_1}{r}$$

We can use our shortcut equation to find the answer:
$$t_{delay} = \frac{d_1 - d_2}{r}$$

Let $r = c$
$$t_{delay} = \frac{8m - 5m}{344.51 m/s}$$

And the answer is
$$t_{delay} = \frac{3m}{\frac{344.51m}{s}}$$

$$t_{delay} = .008708 \, s$$

$$t_{delay} = 8.708 \, ms$$

Finally, just for fun, let's see how close we are to the "1 millisecond per foot" rule. Having established that the distance we're interested in ($d_2 - d_1$) is 3 meters, we make the conversion to feet.

$$1 \, meter = 3.28 \, feet$$

$$3 \times 1 \, meter = 3.28 \, feet \times 3$$

$$3 \, meters = 9.84 \, feet$$

Thus, if we use the "1 millisecond per foot" rule, our answer would be 9.84 ms, which is 1.132 ms more than our answer of 8.708 ms. This might seem like a small difference, but consider a large stadium which would be 100 yards (300 feet) from the stage to the stands:

Problem: What is the difference between the "1 millisecond per foot" rule and an accurate measurement of delay for a distance of 300 feet?

If we use the "1 millisecond per foot" rule for a distance of 300 feet, it should be apparent that the delay would be 300 ms. If we use $d = rt$ instead, then:

$$d = rt$$

$$300 \, ft = 1130 \frac{ft}{s} t$$

$$\frac{300 \, ft \cdot s}{1130 \, ft} = t$$

$$\frac{300 \, ft \cdot s}{1130 \, ft} = t$$

$$\frac{300 \, \cancel{ft} \cdot s}{1130 \, \cancel{ft}} = t$$

$$0.2654 s = t$$

$$265 \, ms = t$$

The difference between these two is 300 ms – 265 ms, or 35 ms. This is definitely an audible difference!

 **More to Know**

In a real situation, you must use your ears to make a judgement call about the quality of your audio, which will also have to do with the acoustics of the venue in which you are setting up your loudspeakers. Since a time difference between two signals will result in acoustic (or electronic) comb filtering, you can have confidence that your answer will be accurate, but also use your ears to decide if the sound is acceptable.

CALCULATING BEATS PER MINUTE AND DELAY

A popular effect used when mixing is to time a delay so that it happens on the beat. Many apps and plug-ins feature a "bpm" setting so that you can dial it without thinking about it. But if you don't have one of those devices handy, you might find a little bit of math can help.

Tempo is set to beats per minute (bpm), but delay times are measured in seconds or milliseconds. This is a simple matter of unit conversion.

> *Problem: If the tempo is 120 bpm, what delay time do you program for a note to occur one beat (quarter note or crotchet) later?*

First, let's get from 120 beats per minute to a number in beats per second. This is something we can determine intuitively: There are 60 seconds in one minute, so if the tempo is 60 bpm you will hear one beat every second, and if the tempo is double that (120 bpm) you will hear two beats every second.

FIGURE 2.8 Wristwatch with seconds and beats

From this we conclude that for 120 bpm, one beat happens every half second (see Figure 2.8 from 6 o'clock to 8 o'clock). So, you would set your delay to 0.5 seconds, or 500 milliseconds.

But what if your tempo is 94 bpm? Let's walk through the steps above and create a mathematical equation. First, convert from minutes to seconds:

120 beats per minute = 120/60 beats per second, and
94 beats per minute = 94/60 beats per second.

Therefore:

$$x \; bpm = \frac{x}{60} \; beats \; per \; second$$

If the tempo is 94 bpm, then

$$94 \; bpm = \frac{94}{60} \; beats \; per \; second$$

$$94 \; bpm = 1.567 \; beats \; per \; second$$

This seems to make sense, because 120 bpm was 2 beats per second, and 94 bpm is slower than that.

We took an additional step when we used 120 bpm as an example: we had to find the amount of time it takes for one beat to happen. In this equation, we know the amount of time for 1.567 beats. So, if at 120 bpm you get 2 beats per second, in order to find the time for one beat we used this equation:

$$x \text{ beats per second} = \frac{\text{seconds}}{x \text{ beats}}$$

Another case where hummingbirds' wings help—it's simply the inverse! So,

$$2 \text{ beats per second} = \frac{1}{2} \text{ second per beat}$$

and

$$1.567 \text{ beats per second} = \frac{1}{1.567} \text{ second per beat}$$

$$.638 \text{ seconds per beat}$$

Your delay time would be set to 638 milliseconds for a quarter note (crotchet).

DIRECT CURRENT AND OHM'S LAW

Direct current describes a nonvarying source of energy, such as an alkaline battery. The voltage remains constant (usually 1.5 volts for a battery) over a long period of time. Ohm's law states that the voltage in a circuit (V) = current (I) × resistance (R), or

$$V = IR$$

Problem: If R equals 5Ω and I equals 2A, what is the voltage of the circuit?

Recall that $V = IR$. By simply "plugging in" the values, we obtain

$$V = 5\,\Omega \cdot 2A$$

$$V = 10 \text{ Volts}$$

Figure 2.9 shows a different example using a simple circuit:

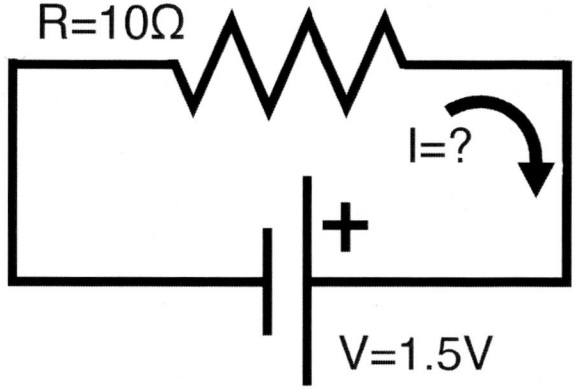

FIGURE 2.9 A simple DC circuit

So if you know the voltage and resistance, you can calculate a value for the current. In Figure 2.9, the voltage is 1.5 V and the resistance is 10 Ω. Therefore, to find the current, use Ohm's law as follows:

$$V = IR$$

$$I = \frac{V}{R}$$

$$I = \frac{1.5V}{10\Omega}$$

$$I = .15\ A$$

(Your audio or electronics text will describe how ohms and amperes become volts.)

POWER EQUATIONS

Another equation you will come across in audio is one for power, which resembles Ohm's law:

$$P = IV$$

But what if you don't know the value for current? Or what if you aren't told what the voltage is? One important trick you can do with algebra is *substitution*. You can still find the power used by a circuit if all you know is the resistance and the voltage. In the equation $V = IR$, you can solve for current (hint: do you remember how to set up the equation using a triangle as we did for $c = \lambda f$ and $d = rt$?).

$$V = IR$$

$$I = \frac{V}{R}$$

Power equals current times resistance, so you can substitute this number in the power law equation:

$$P = IV$$

$$P = \left(\frac{V}{R}\right)V$$

$$P = \frac{V^2}{R}$$

Exercise 2-2

a. *Determine how to find power using only current (I) and resistance (R) without using volts (V).*

b. *How much power is dissipated in a circuit where a 120 V source produces 1.5 amps across a 25 Ω resistor?*

See the solutions at end of book.

ALTERNATING CURRENT

Alternating current (AC) is familiar to you as the electricity that "comes out of the wall." It feeds our lamps, stoves, televisions, and so forth. In the United States AC runs at 60 Hz, and in Europe it runs at 50 Hz. The voltage is a (somewhat) constant 120 V in North America and parts of South America, while in Europe it can range from 240 V in the UK to 220 V for mainland Europe and parts of Asia and Africa. (You can search the Internet for maps of voltages by country.)

Audio is a type of alternating current, where the amplitude of the wave is measured in volts. Figure 2.10 shows the difference between alternating current (AC) and direct current (DC).

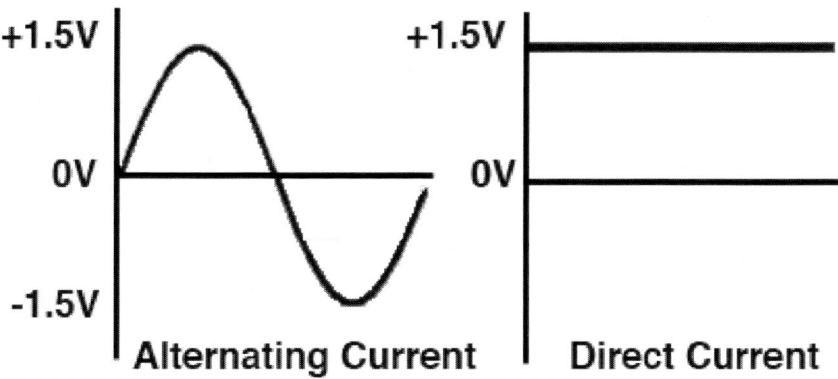

FIGURE 2.10 Alternating current and direct current

Because the waveform of an alternating current is ever changing, electronic circuits have more complex equations than Ohm's law. Components such as inductors and capacitors behave differently based on the frequency of the incoming signal. So instead of resistance, we must refer *impedance* (denoted by Z), which is kind of like a frequency-dependent resistance.

Impedance of an Inductor

Here are some examples. In a circuit with an inductor, the impedance (frequency-dependent resistance) is measured by this equation:

$$Z_L = 2\pi f L$$

FIGURE 2.11 AC circuit with one inductor

In Figure 2.11, the frequency is 10 Hz, and the inductance is one Henry (H). Thus, the inductive impedance of the circuit would be

$$Z_L = 2\pi f L$$
$$Z_L = 2\pi \cdot 10 \cdot 1H$$
$$Z_L = 20\pi$$
$$Z_L = 62.83 \Omega$$

The higher the inductance, the higher the resistance of the circuit.

Impedance of a Capacitor

In a circuit with a capacitor, the impedance is measured by this equation:

$$Z_C = \frac{1}{2\pi f C}$$

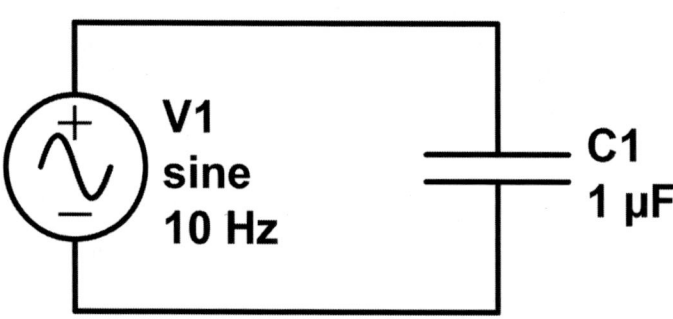

FIGURE 2.12 AC circuit with one capacitor

In Figure 2.12, the frequency is 10 Hz and the capacitor has a value of 1μF. Thus, the impedance of the circuit would be

$$Z_C = \frac{1}{2\pi f C}$$

$$Z_C = \frac{1}{2\pi 10 \cdot 0.000001F}$$

$$Z_C = \frac{1}{2\pi \cdot 00001F}$$

$$Z_C = \frac{1}{0.00006283F}$$

$$Z_C = 15915.49 \Omega$$

or 15.915 kΩ. That is a pretty high resistance for the same low frequency we had in the example with the inductor. Keep in mind how inverse proportions work: as the frequency gets higher, the impedance caused by the capacitor will decrease!

Capacitors in Audio Circuits

The design of electronic audio circuits is beyond the scope of this book. However, I would like to cover one concept that can often be confusing to students: how does an inductor or capacitor affect the audio path in a series or parallel circuit? Allow me to introduce . . . the elephant (Figure 2.13) and the mouse (Figure 2.14).

FIGURE 2.13 Elephant

FIGURE 2.14 Mouse

I like to think of a capacitor as an "elephant hunter." It hunts and cages (stores) anything large—such as the long wavelengths of low frequencies. A capacitor stores energy, especially at low frequencies, depending on the value of the capacitor (measured in Farads (F), microFarads (μF), and even nanoFarads (nF).

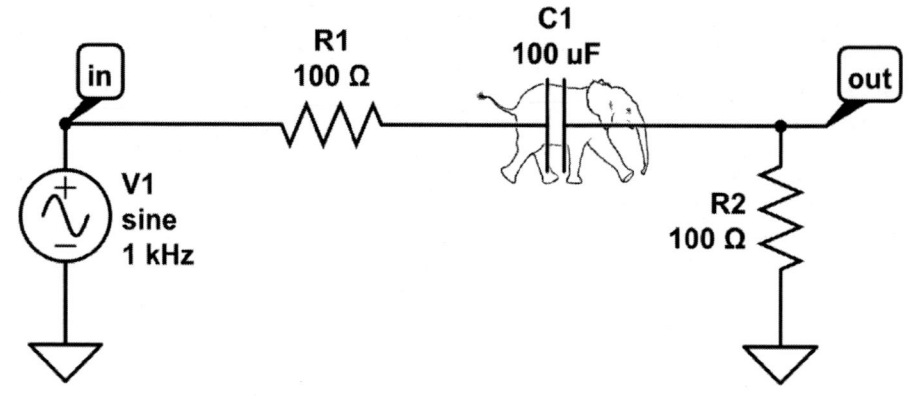

FIGURE 2.15 Capacitor in series with audio signal (diagram made using CircuitLab.com)

So, for my analogy, when looking at a capacitor in series with a circuit, you can see that the elephant has no choice but to be trapped by C1, and only the smaller, higher "mouselike" frequencies get through. Audio engineers learn to recognize the filter in Figure 2.16 as a "high pass" filter.

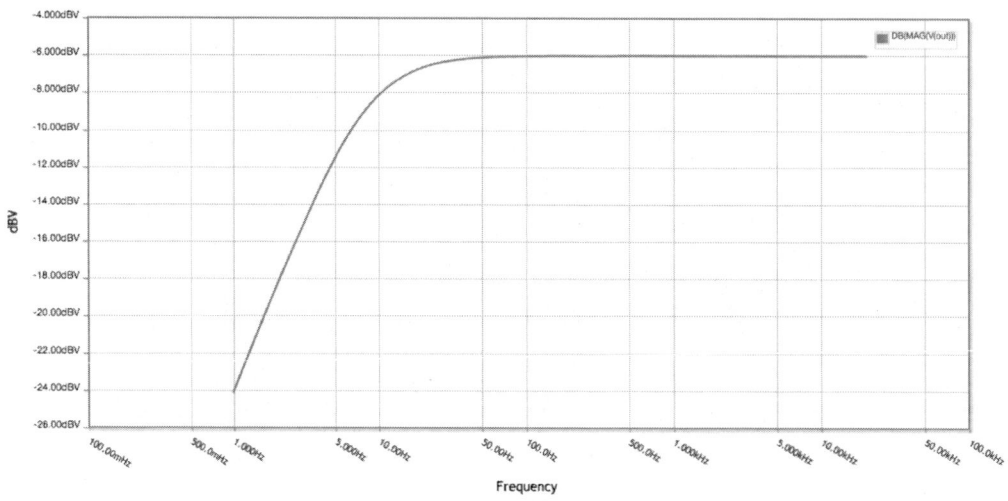

FIGURE 2.16 High pass filter created with capacitor in series (diagram made using CircuitLab.com)

In a circuit where the capacitor is in *parallel* with the output, the elephants (low frequencies) have a choice: they can avoid the "hunt and cage" capacitor by "running away" to escape through the rest of the circuit where the "load resistor" (R2) is (Figure 2.17). On the other hand, higher frequencies are not afraid of the "elephant hunter" and prefer the path of least resistance. Those high frequencies are diverted *away* from the resistor and go through the capacitor instead, which offers them no resistance at all! Audio engineers learn to recognize Figure 2.18 as a "low pass" filter.

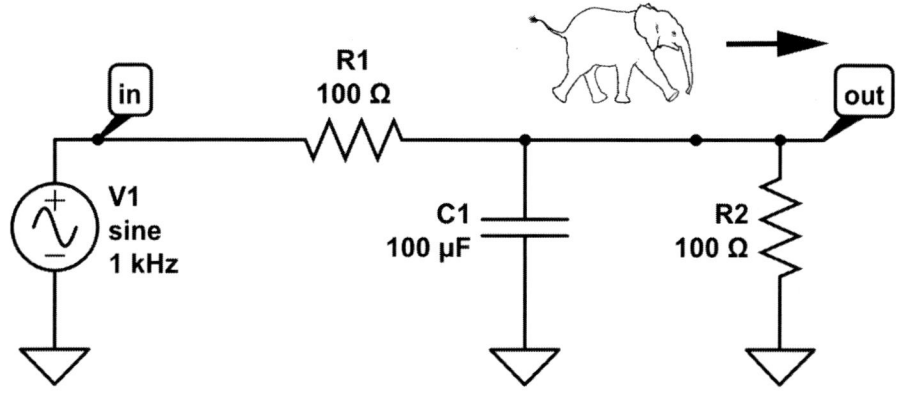

FIGURE 2.17 Capacitor in parallel with audio signal (diagram made using CircuitLab.com)

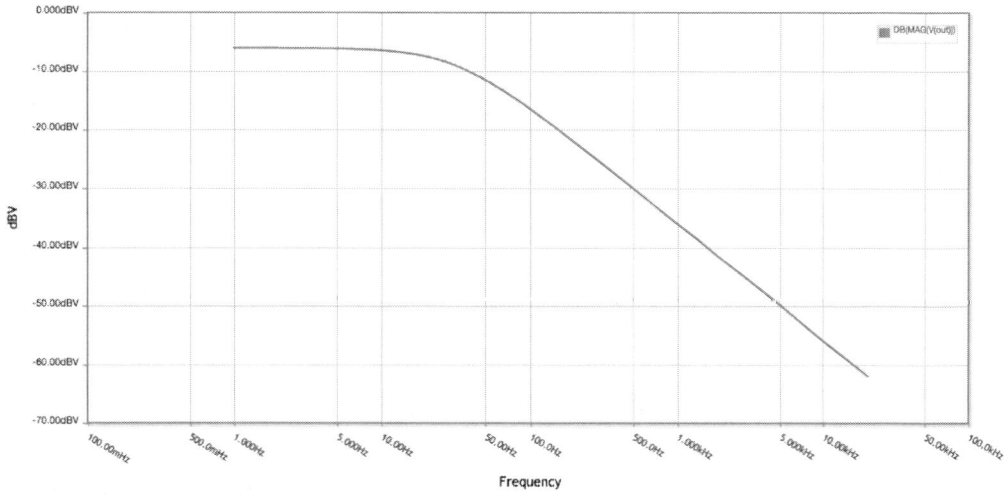

FIGURE 2.18 Low pass filter created with capacitor in parallel (diagrams made using CircuitLab.com)

In the equation $Z_C = \frac{1}{2\pi f C}$, a low frequency might be 1 Hz or 10 Hz or even 50 Hz. Let's assume capacitance will be 1 Farad—just so we can see the effect of changing the frequency. For a low frequency (10 Hz), the impedance is

$$Z_C = \frac{1}{2\pi \cdot 10 \cdot 1} = 7.927 \Omega$$

which is close to 8 Ω. But for a high frequency—for example 10 kHz:

$$Z_C = \frac{1}{2\pi \cdot 10{,}000 \cdot 1}$$

$$Z_C = 0.0000159 \Omega$$

which is .01 milliohms—the resistance is a very tiny amount. This means that the higher the frequency, the lower the resistance. And since current "follows the path of least resistance," the higher frequencies will "prefer" to follow the path with the capacitor in it. It's invisible to the little "mouselike" frequencies—almost like a short-circuit—but a barrier to the big "elephant" frequencies.

Inductors in Audio Circuits

If capacitors are "elephant hunters," then an inductor is a "mouse hunter."

$$Z_L = 2\pi f L$$

If we have a value for inductance of one Henry, then we can play with frequencies again. A low frequency of 50 Hz means

$$Z_L = 2\pi \cdot 50 \cdot 1$$

$$Z_L = 314.16 \, \Omega$$

or around 314 Ω, a considerable amount of impedance. A high frequency of 10,000 Hz means

$$Z_L = 2\pi \cdot 10{,}000 \cdot 1$$

$$Z_L = 62{,}831.85 \, \Omega$$

The higher the frequency, the more the impedance. In a circuit with an inductor placed in series of the audio (Figure 2.19) high frequencies are "caught," so the resulting frequency response is low-pass (Figure 2.20).

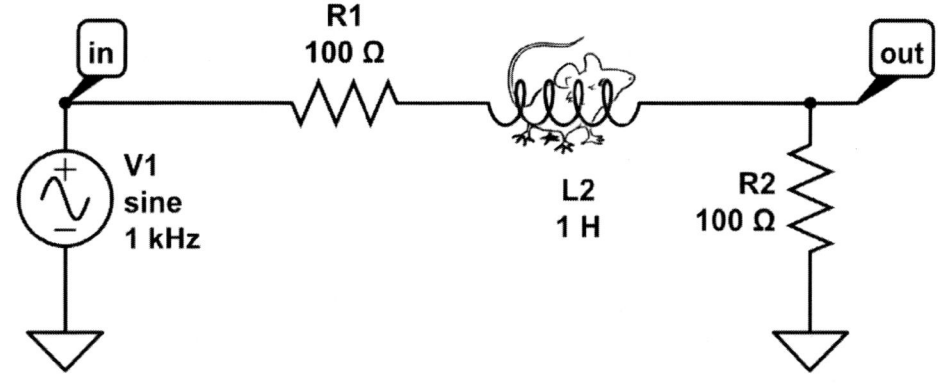

FIGURE 2.19 Inductor in series with audio signal

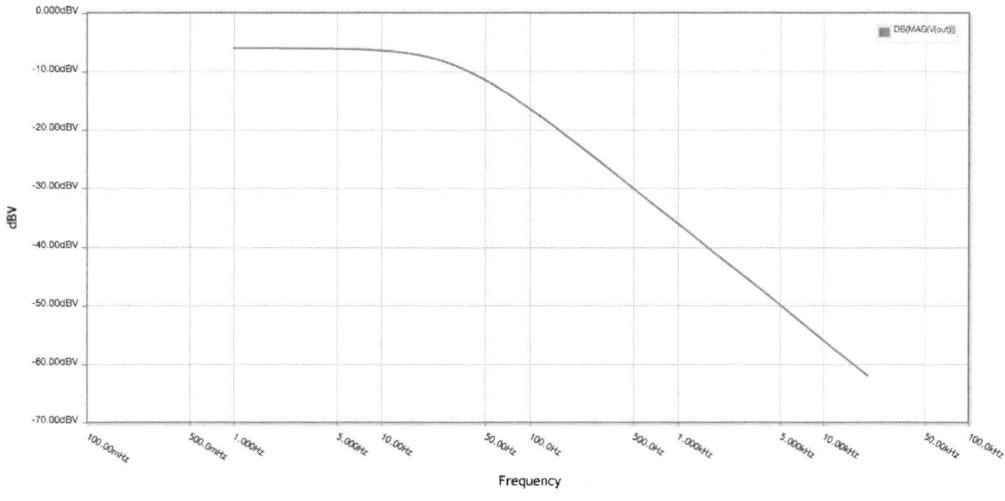

FIGURE 2.20 Low pass filter created with an inductor in series (diagram made using CircuitLab.com)

In a circuit where the inductor is in parallel with the audio output, the "mouselike" high frequencies run away from the "hunter" and are instead redirected to the load. Thus, it is a high-pass filter (Figure 2.21).

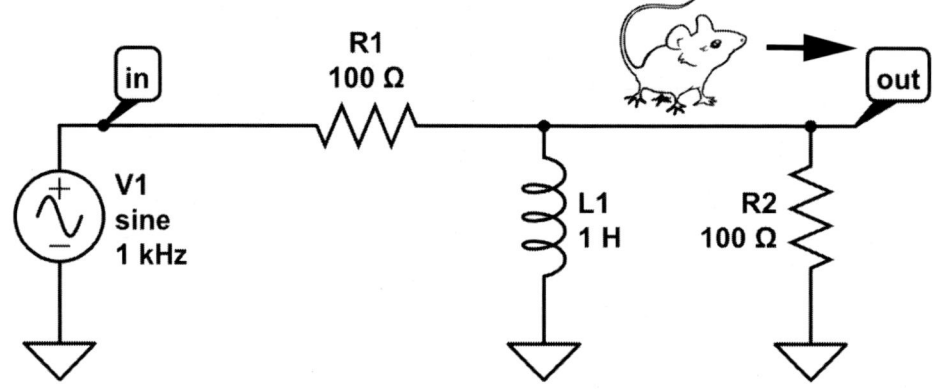

FIGURE 2.21 Inductor in parallel with audio signal (diagrams made using CircuitLab.com)

Resonant Circuits

In a circuit with both an inductor and a capacitor, a **resonant frequency** is created. It is denoted by f_c (center frequency) and given by

$$f_c = \frac{1}{2\pi\sqrt{LC}}$$

A resonance can be used to enhance or reduce certain frequencies. You would recognize this as a "peak/dip" curve in a parametric equalizer.

 More to Know

The Analog Sound

Engineers are fond of capturing that "analog sound." Whenever inductors or capacitors are used, the timing of certain parts of the signal are being affected by phase shift. Because it takes time for a capacitor or inductor to "store" (that is, hunt and trap) a signal, part of the audio will lead or lag behind the rest. Lead/lag refers to the relationship between current and voltage in these components. The *entire* audio signal will always be delayed through each component.

THREE
Audio and Logarithms

RATIOS

If you have used compressors, you have probably seen the term "ratios." They can be found in many other places as well. For example, did you know that in the United States, the ratio of men to women working professionally in the field of audio engineering is 20 to 1?[1] There are a few ways to express this statistic:

- For every woman working professionally in the field of audio, there are twenty men
- For every one hundred men working professionally in the field of audio, there are five women
- Five percent of people working professionally in the field of audio are women.

Maybe you can also see that

$$1:20 = \frac{1}{20} = .05 = 5\%$$

In this way, ratios are useful for expressing large numbers. If the number of working professionals in audio in the United States is, say, 25,000, then the number of women is 1,250. Let's talk about another way ratios are useful using an example which is your favorite and mine, the compressor.

COMPRESSION RATIOS

You see them on almost every compressor or limiter plugin: the "ratio" button, usually with a range from 1:1 to ∞:1. In the last chapter we saw the graph of $y = x$. This is the same graph; for each dB of input we get the same dB of output.

FIGURE 3.1 Pro Tools Compressor with ratio set to 1:1

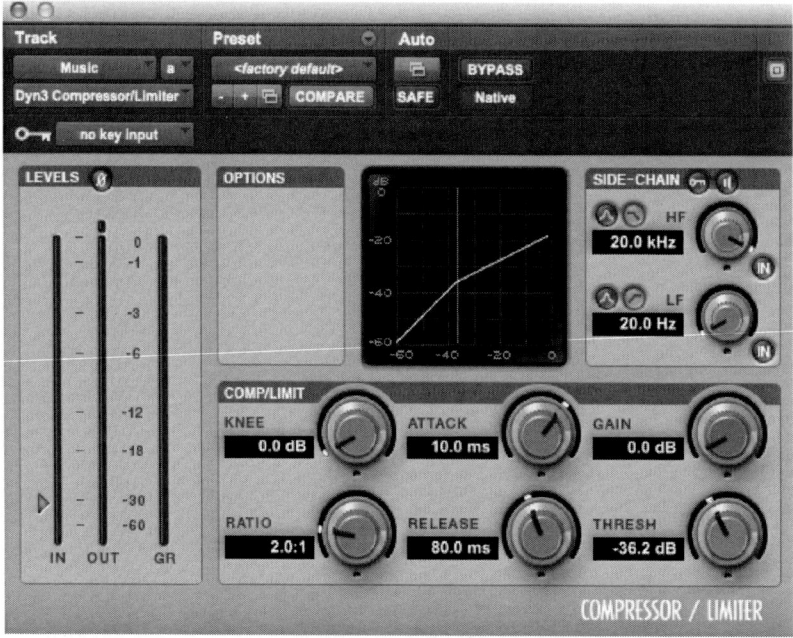

FIGURE 3.2 Pro Tools Compressor with 2:1 ratio

Compare Figure 3.2 to the graph of $y = \dfrac{x}{2}$.

But in this graph, there is a "bend" in the graph (sometimes called a "knee"): the graph corresponds to $y = x$ for the first part of the graph. Then, at the threshold (or "knee"), the graph changes to $y = \dfrac{x}{2}$.

You might describe this by saying, "What comes out is what goes in, but only up to the threshold point" (−36.2 dBFS in this figure). After that, you only get "half of what you put in." Or, for every 2 that go in, only one comes out (2 to 1).

Notice that −20 dBFS on the vertical (input) axis roughly intersects with −10 dBFS on the horizontal (output) axis, but not exactly. Why is that? If the ratio is 2 to 1, shouldn't −20 line up with −10? Keep in mind that it's only 2:1 after a certain point. So consider the graph below, which shows three equations:

$$y = x,$$

$$y = \frac{x}{2},$$

and

$$y = 2 + \frac{x}{2}.$$

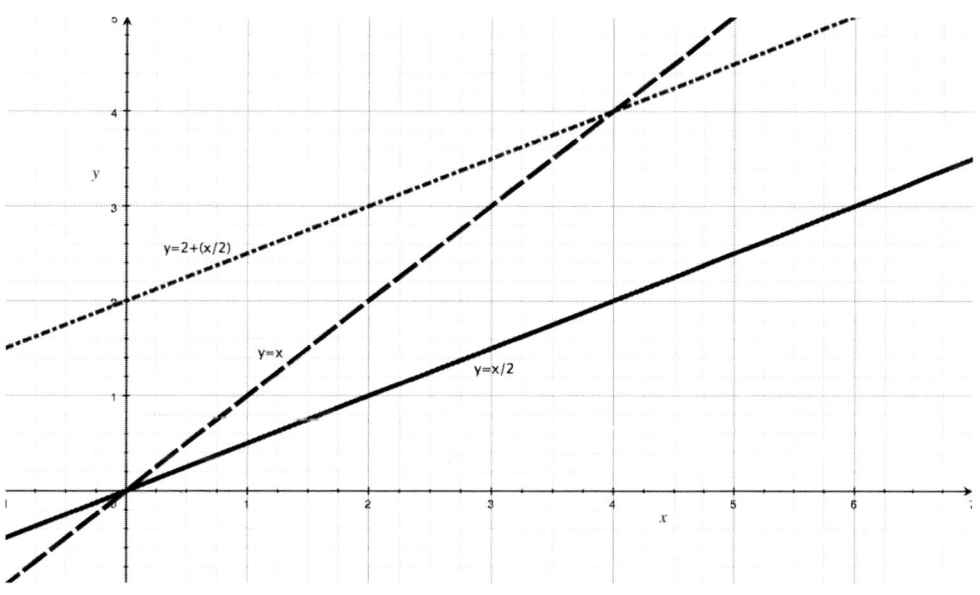

FIGURE 3.3 Graphs of $y = x$, $y = x/2$, and $y = 2 + (x/2)$

In the graph $y = x$, the points $x = 4$ and $y = 4$ intersect at (4,4). For $y = x/2$, $x = 4$ intersects with $y = 2$ at (4,2) because

$$y = \frac{x}{2},$$

$$y = \frac{4}{2},$$

$$y = 2.$$

But if we *add* 2 at the beginning $(2 + \frac{x}{2})$, notice how the graph shifts upward. For $x = 4$,

$$y = 2 + \frac{x}{2},$$

$$y = 2 + \frac{4}{2},$$

$$y = 2 + 2,$$

$$y = 4.$$

So, in our example with the compressor, if the input and output are equal to a certain point (i.e., the "threshold"), it's like shifting the graph upwards.

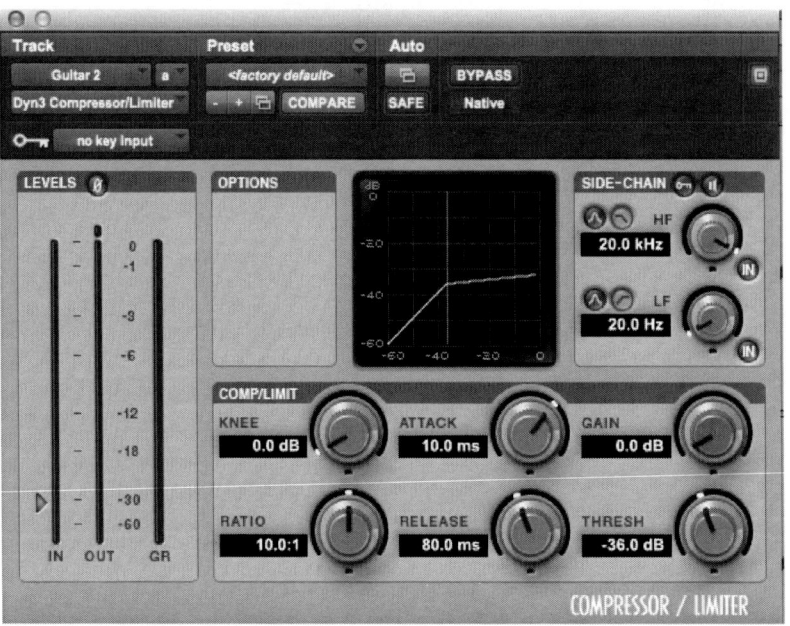

FIGURE 3.4 Pro Tools Compressor with 10:1 ratio

In Figure 3.4, starting at −36 dBFS you only get a *tenth* of what you put in. This is a 10:1 ratio, which many textbooks will tell you counts as "limiting."

DECIBELS

The softest sound a human ear can detect is very, very small. If you have every been tormented by a mosquito, you are well aware of this. (Mosquito wings are very thin and tiny!) Sound energy is measured in a unit known as the Pascal (abbreviated Pa). 1 Pa is equivalent to the energy required to change atmospheric pressure by a factor of one. The amount of energy perceived when standing next to a jet engine is around 100 Pa, and this is commonly referred to as the loudest sound humans can physically withstand—also known as the "threshold of pain"!

The softest sound we can hear—even softer than a mosquito's wings beating[2]—is 20 microPascals (20μPa, which can also be represented as .000020 Pa). So what is the ratio between the loudest and softest sounds we can hear? A ratio can be written as $a:b$. If a = 100 Pa and b = .000020 Pa, then

$$100\ Pa : .000020\ Pa =$$

$$\frac{100}{.000020} =$$

$$5{,}000{,}000$$

Using ratios is a wonderful way for us to describe the softest and loudest sounds we can hear. But 5 million is still a huge number. Fortunately, we have a unit of measurement that can break that number down even further. The deci**Bel** (commonly written as "decibel" but abbreviated dB) is a unit of measure that is calculated by taking the ratio of two numbers.

$$decibel = 10 \cdot \log\frac{A}{B}$$

In the example of loudest and softest sound, we can use the softest sound as a "reference" value in the denominator. Choosing a reference is a crucial step when using decibels. Your reference determines whether you are measuring decibels in volts (dBV) or millivolts (dBmv), sound pressure levels (dB SPL), or full-scale levels in digital systems (dBFS).

POWER VERSUS VOLTAGE (LOGARITHMS AND EXPONENTS)

Now, it brings me no pleasure to throw a complication in here. Once you've grasped the intention to make big numbers smaller and more manageable, I have to mention that working with certain values means applying a little—you guessed it—math. Let's have a look at sound intensity (I). It is described as *Power* divided by *Area:*

$$I = \frac{P}{A}$$

Since sound propagates in a sphere (see "Geometry of a sphere," ch. 5, p. 94–95), the formula can also be written as

$$I = \frac{P}{4\pi r^2}$$

Whenever the values in a logarithmic equation are squared, we have to follow this rule:

$$\log A^x = x \cdot \log A$$

So in the case of our intensity values

$$decibel = 10 \cdot \log \frac{I_1}{I_2}$$

$$decibel = 10 \cdot \log \left(\frac{\frac{P}{A_1}}{\frac{P}{A_2}} \right)$$

$$decibel = 10 \cdot \log \left(\frac{P}{4\pi r_1} \cdot \frac{4\pi r_2}{P} \right)$$

The "like" terms can be crossed out, giving

$$decibel = 10 \cdot \log \left(\frac{P}{4\pi r_1^2} \cdot \frac{4\pi r_2^2}{P} \right)$$

$$decibel = 10 \cdot \log \left(\frac{r_2^2}{r_1^2} \right)$$

$$\log A^x = x \cdot \log A$$

We can move the exponent out, so if

$$\log A^x = x \cdot \log A$$

then

$$\log A^2 = 2 \cdot \log A$$

and the equation for finding an answer in decibels with squared terms becomes

$$decibel = 10 \cdot \log (\frac{A}{B})^2$$

$$decibel = 20 \cdot \log (\frac{A}{B})$$

There is sometimes confusion when deciding if a decibel equation begins with "10 log" or a "20 log" expression. The general rule of thumb is if you are working with sound, voltage, or anything which starts off with a squared term, begin with 20 × log. Thus, when working with Pascals, the equation is

$$decibel = 20 \cdot \log \frac{100Pa}{.000020Pa}$$

$$decibel = 20 \cdot \log 5{,}000{,}000$$

$$decibel = 20 \cdot 6.7$$

$$decibel = 134 \text{ dB}$$

So the range of human hearing is about 134 dB, and 134 dB is often referred to as the "threshold of pain" (also called the "threshold of sensation")!

Antilogs

Consider the following:

Problem: Given a reference voltage of 1.25 V, what voltage is 10 dB more?

As mentioned above, it is necessary to choose a reference (such as 1.25 V) when working with decibels. For this one, the equation is

$$10dB = 20\log \frac{x}{1.25V}$$

So how do we solve for x? We need to compute the *antilog* of the number. First, we will solve for as much as we can. Recall that

$$\log \frac{A}{B} = \log A - \log B$$

$$10dB = 20(\log x - \log 1.25V)$$

$$\frac{10}{20} = \log x - \log 1.25v$$

$$0.5 + \log 1.25 = \log x$$

$$0.5 + 0.0969 = \log x$$

$$0.5969 = \log x$$

So now we are stuck: how do we solve for x? One way is to remember the point of using logarithms: to take powers of 10 and put them in a useful scale. So,

$$\log 10{,}000{,}000 = 7 \, .$$

Another way of thinking about this is that there are seven zeroes in the number 10 million:

$$10^7 = 10{,}000{,}000$$

You could say, "The log of a number is the power to which 10 must be raised to get that number." For example, "The log of 100 is the exponent of 10 that gives you 100." Ten to the power of 2 is 100, so the log of 100 is 2.

So, back to our problem: "The log of 0.5969 is the exponent of 10 that gives you 0.5969." Or, "Ten to the power of what is 0.5969?"

$$10^x = 0.5969$$

is the same as writing

$$0.5969 = \log x$$

To solve for x, you need the antilog function. On a calculator, the antilog button is shown as 10^x. To find the antilog, enter 0.5969 and hit the 10^x button.

$$antilog\ 0.5969 = x$$

$$3.9528 = x$$

This means that 3.9528 volts is 10 dB more than 1.25 volts.

The VU Problem

VU stands for "Voltage Unit." You will recognize a VU meter as an "analog meter" that uses a needle, as in Figure 3.5.

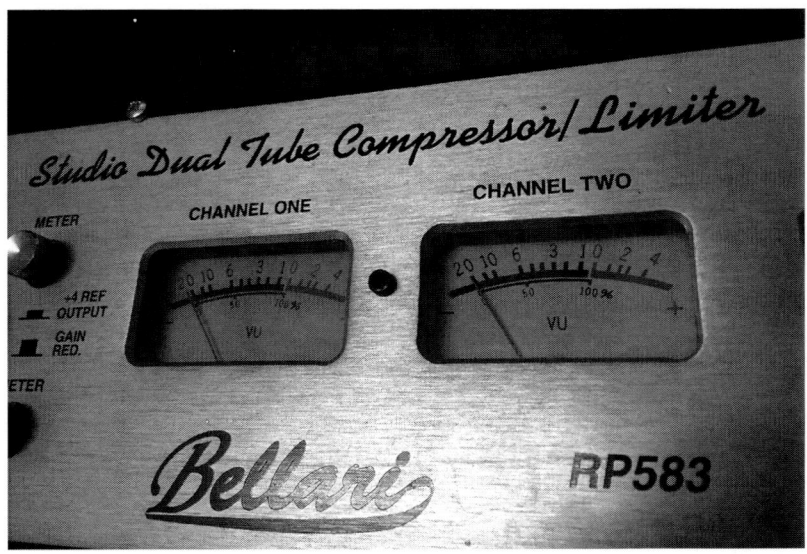

FIGURE 3.5 A VU Meter

Consider the following:

> *Problem: A tone on channel 1 is panned hard left and reads 0 VU with the fader at unity. That tone is then muted. A second tone on channel 2 with the same volume is also panned hard left and set to read 0 VU with the fader at unity. What will the meter read when channel 1 and channel 2 are unmuted?*

Before we solve this problem, a little intuition might help. You might already know that the needle will go up. But how far? This is not a situation where 0 + 0 = 0! What's your guess?

1. 1.5 VU
2. 3.01 VU
3. 4.5 VU
4. 6.02 VU

The answer is #4: 6.02 VU. Why? It will help to know that your reference of 0 VU isn't really "0". It's really 1.228 V_{RMS}. (The RMS stands for Root Mean Squared; more in chapter 7, p. 109.) The equation for adding the voltages is

$$dB = 10 \log \frac{V_1^2}{V_2^2}$$

Recall that the squared terms can be moved out:

$$dB = 20\log\frac{V_1}{V_2}$$

So the two channels at 0 VU are actually at 1.228 volts, and are being referenced to 1.228 volts.

$$dB = 20\log\frac{1.228V + 1.228V}{1.228V}$$

$$dB = 20\log 2$$

$$dB = 6.02$$

Thus, the left channel's VU meter will read 6.02 dB.

We found a magic number

POWERS OF TWO AND BINARY NUMBERS

The resolution of a PCM (Pulse Code Modulated) system is described by how many bits it uses. A 16-bit system has a resolution of 65,536 (or 2^{16}) "steps." Here is a table showing powers of two:

Power of two	Decimal equivalent	Power of two	Decimal equivalent
2^0	1	2^9	512
2^1	2	2^{10}	1,024
2^2	4	2^{11}	2,048
2^3	8	2^{12}	4,096
2^4	16	2^{13}	8,192
2^5	32	2^{14}	16,384
2^6	64	2^{15}	32,768
2^7	128	2^{16}	65,536
2^8	256	2^{17}	131,072

TABLE 3.1 Powers of two and their decimal equivalents

The following table shows values in each "place" of a binary number.

2^7	2^6	2^5	2^4	2^3	2^2	2^1	2^0
0 or 128	0 or 64	0 or 32	0 or 16	0 or 8	0 or 4	0 or 2	0 or 1

TABLE 3.2 Building a binary number

Problem: What decimal number is represented by the binary number 10011010?

To solve this problem, we put each of the digits in the number into the first table (in the appropriate "power of two" cell). If the number is 0, we write a 0 in the next table. If the number is a 1, we write the value associated with that power of two, as follows:

2^7	2^6	2^5	2^4	2^3	2^2	2^1	2^0
1	0	0	1	1	0	1	0

2^7	2^6	2^5	2^4	2^3	2^2	2^1	2^0
128	0	0	16	8	0	2	0

Then we add the numbers together:

$$128 + 0 + 0 + 16 + 8 + 0 + 2 + 0 = 154$$

Exercise 3-1

Solve for the following binary numbers (you can use the practice grids below, the first one has been filled in for you):

a) 011
b) 10001110101
c) 11111

a)

2^7	2^6	2^5	2^4	2^3	2^2	2^1	2^0
					0	1	1

b)

2^7	2^6	2^5	2^4	2^3	2^2	2^1	2^0

c)

2^7	2^6	2^5	2^4	2^3	2^2	2^1	2^0

As a bonus, work out the decimal equivalent of this 16-bit number:

1111 1111 1111 1111

See the solutions at end of book.

Connecting Components

Sine waves ascend in a positive direction ($y > 0$) and descend in a negative direction ($y < 0$). So a question you might have is, How does that work in binary? What number represents the "zero crossing," and how do you get negative numbers?

One way binary systems handle negative numbers is with a mathematical function called "two's complement." First, the value is flipped with a Boolean NOT gate. So wherever there is a 0 it is replaced with a 1, and vice versa. For example, the number 001 would be 110. Then the number 1 is added to the result.

More to Know

Here is an overview of logic gates and associate truth tables:

"AND"			"OR"			"NOT"	
input1	input2	output	input1	input2	output	input	output
1	1	1	1	1	1	1	0
0	0	0	0	0	0	0	1
1	0	0	1	0	1		
0	1	0	0	1	1		

TABLE 3.3 AND, OR, and NOT gates

If you have two bits arriving at an AND gate, and they are both "1", then "1" is passed along by the AND gate. The logic can be written as English expressions as: For an AND gate, "If both expressions equal 1, then the output is 1." For an OR gate, "If either expression equals 1, then the output is 1."

In Table 3.4, look at the number 3, then find –3. The binary value of 3 is 011. If you flip the numbers, it becomes 100. Finally, add a 1 and you will see the 2's complement value is 101, or –3.

3-bit two's-complement integers		
Bits	Unsigned value	2's complement value
011	3	3
010	2	2
001	1	1
000	0	0
111	7	-1
110	6	-2
101	5	-3

TABLE 3.4 3-bit values with decimal and 2's complement values[3]

NOTES

1. Women's Audio Mission, accessed 27 December 2015, http://www.womensaudiomission.org.

2. Pete R. Jones, "What's the Quietest Sound a Human Can Hear? (A.k.a. 'Why Omega-3 Fatty Acids Might Not Cure Dyslexia')," Dr. Pete R. Jones's website, November 20, 2014, accessed 27 December 2015, http://www.ucl.ac.uk/~smgxprj/public/askscience_v1_8.pdf.

3. Bob Pusateri, "Signed Integer Ranges: Why and How," *Bob Pusateri: SQL Server and Kindred Subjects* (blog), February 26, 2015, accessed 17 July 2015, http://www.bobpusateri.com/archive/2015/02/signed-integer-ranges-why-and-how.

FOUR
Reading Graphs

LOCATING COORDINATES

In order to read frequency response curves, waveform displays, and microphone response patterns on a polar plot, it's important to know how to read various graphs.

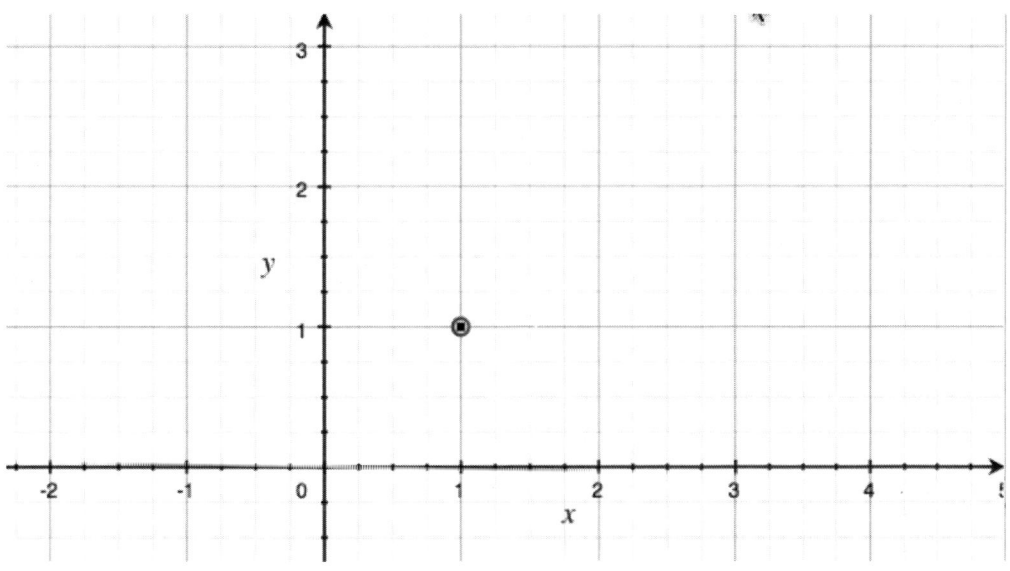

FIGURE 4.1 Graph of the point (1,1)

To find a single point on a graph, you are usually given coordinates in an (x,y) format. For example, to find the point (1,1), you locate 1 on the x axis and draw a vertical line (x = 1), and then locate 1 on the y axis and draw a horizontal line. The point where these two lines intersect is (1,1) (Figure 4.1).

Exercise 4-1

Plot these points using the graph below:

a) (5,3)
b) (2,-1)
c) (-5,-5)
d) (-4,3)

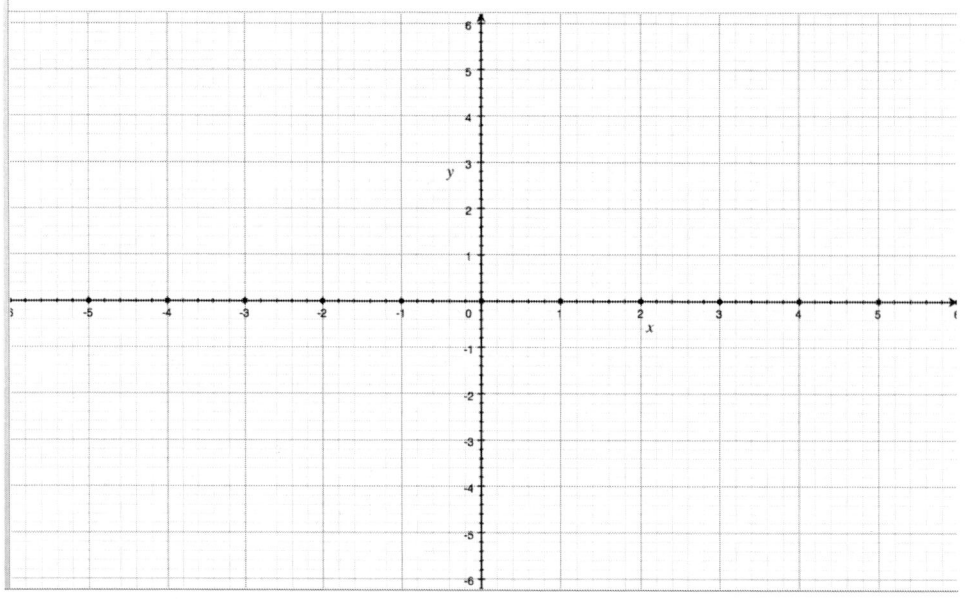

FIGURE 4.2 Blank graph

See solutions at end of book.

GRAPHING FUNCTIONS

Cartesian Graphs

A function is usually written like this:

$$f(x) = 2 + 3x$$

The term *f(x)* can also be substituted with a *y*:

$$y = 2 + 3x$$

Let's look at how to graph this by examining each term.

Figure 4.3 is a graph of the equation $y = 2$

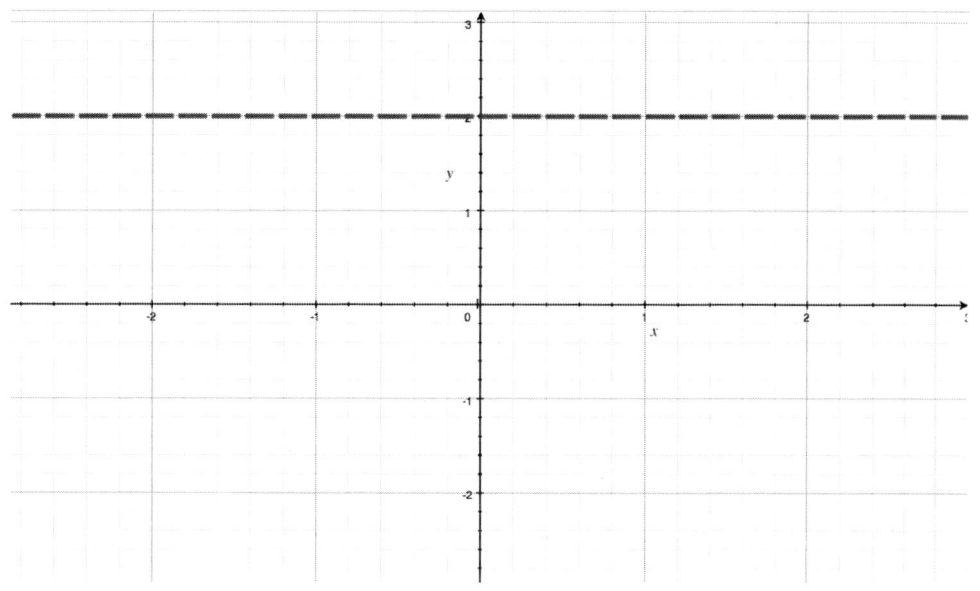

FIGURE 4.3   The graph $y = 2$

You would draw a horizontal line through the number 2 on the *y* axis. Figure 4.4 graphs the equation $y = x$.

84 MATH FUNDAMENTALS FOR AUDIO

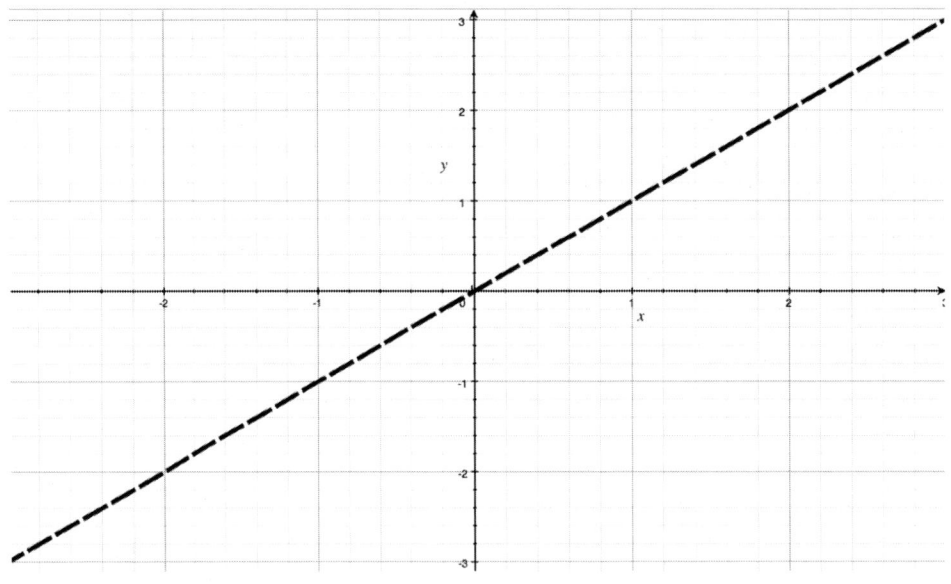

FIGURE 4.4 The graph $y = x$

Then, for every value of y, there is an equal value of x: (0,0), (1,1), (25,25), and so forth. If y happened to be negative, x would also be negative: (-5,-5), for example.

What about $y = 3x$? Well, if $x = 1$, $y = 3$. If $x = 2$, $y = (3 \times 2) = 6$, and so on, like this:

for $x = 0$, $y = 0$ and has the coordinates (0,0)

$$y = (3 \cdot 0)$$
$$y = 0$$

for $x = 1$, $y = 3$ and has the coordinates (1,3)

$$y = 3 \cdot 1$$
$$y = 3$$

for $x = 2$, $y = 6$ and has the coordinates (2,6)

$$y = 3 \cdot 2$$
$$y = 6$$

for $x = 3$, $y = 9$ and has the coordinates (3,9)

$$y = 3 \cdot 3$$
$$y = 9$$

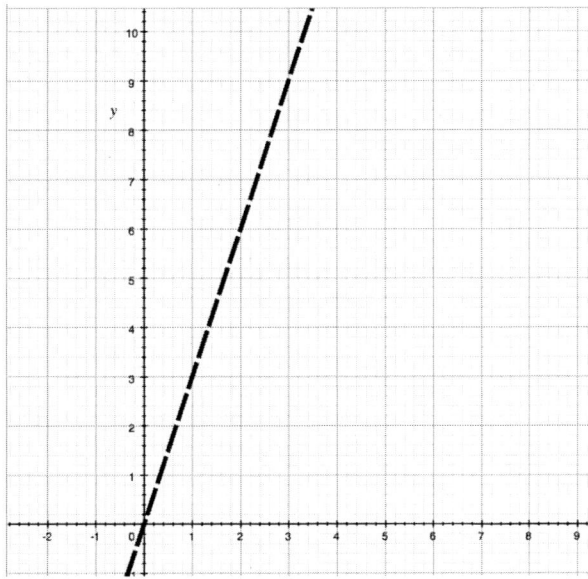

FIGURE 4.5 The graph $y = 3x$

So, let's have a look at our original equation, equation 4-1.

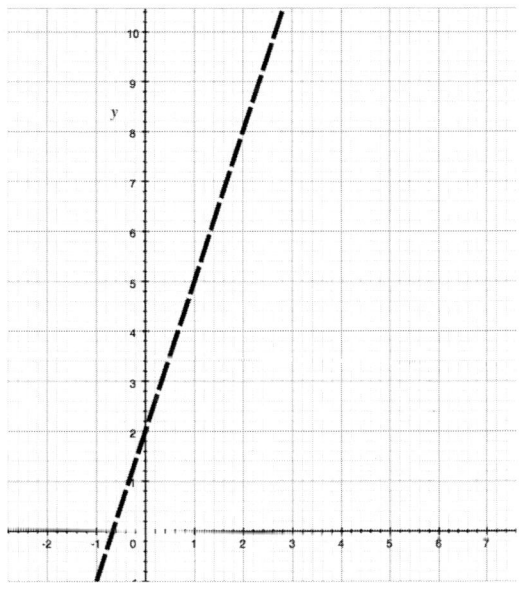

FIGURE 4.6 The graph $y = 2 + 3x$

You can see that the graph in Figure 4.6 has a similar shape to $y = x$. However, instead of crossing through (0,0), the graph starts at $y = 2$ and is a little steeper. Look again at equation 4-1.

Then for $x = 0$, $y = 2$ or (0,2)

$$y = 2 + 3 \cdot 0 = 2$$

$x = 1$, $y = 5$ or (1,5)

$$y = 2 + 3 \cdot 1 = 5$$

$x = 2$, $y = 8$ or (2,8)

$$y = 2 + 3 \cdot 2 = 8$$

$x = 3$, $y = 11$ or (3,11)

$$y = 2 + 3 \cdot 3 = 11$$

… and so on.

Exercise 4-2

a) Graph $y = \frac{x}{2}$

b) Graph $y = \frac{x}{10}$

Linear Graphs

Linear graphs can be used for visualizing small numbers or big numbers. In Figure 4.7, you can see that Nancy's Nissan does pretty decent business and sells anywhere from 30 to 110 cars a month. If the graph can accommodate numbers up to 120 by using increments of 20, it's easy to visualize how they are doing.

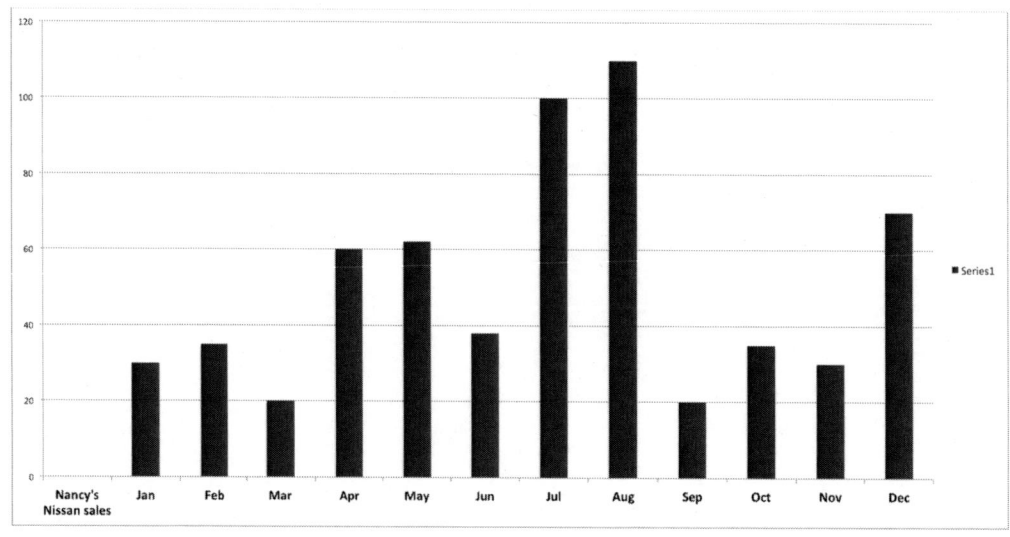

FIGURE 4.7 A linear graph showing car sales at a single dealership

In Figure 4.8, we have to change the scale to accommodate thousands of cars sold.

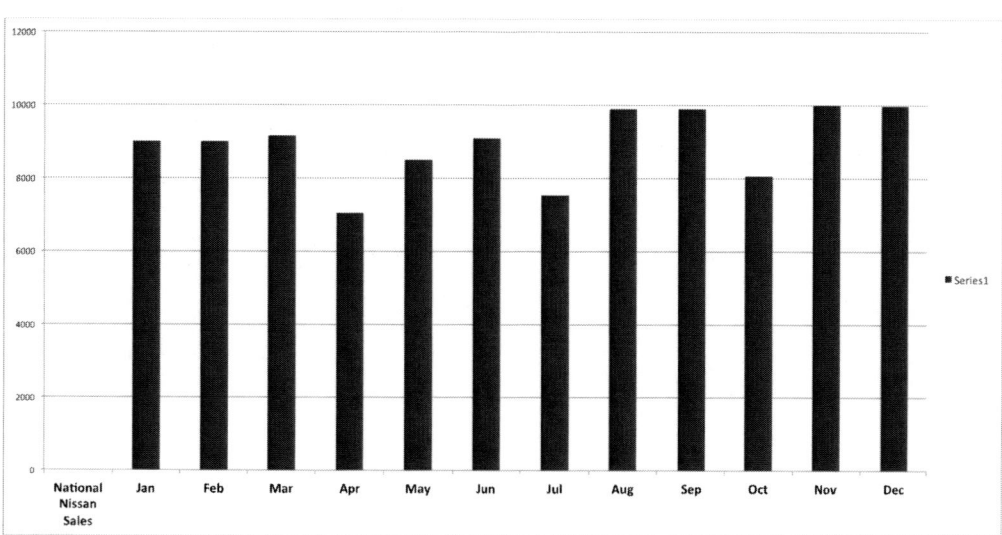

FIGURE 4.8 A linear graph showing thousands of cars sold nationwide

A waveform display is a type of linear graph: it shows the amplitude of audio along a uniform time scale (see Figure 4.9).

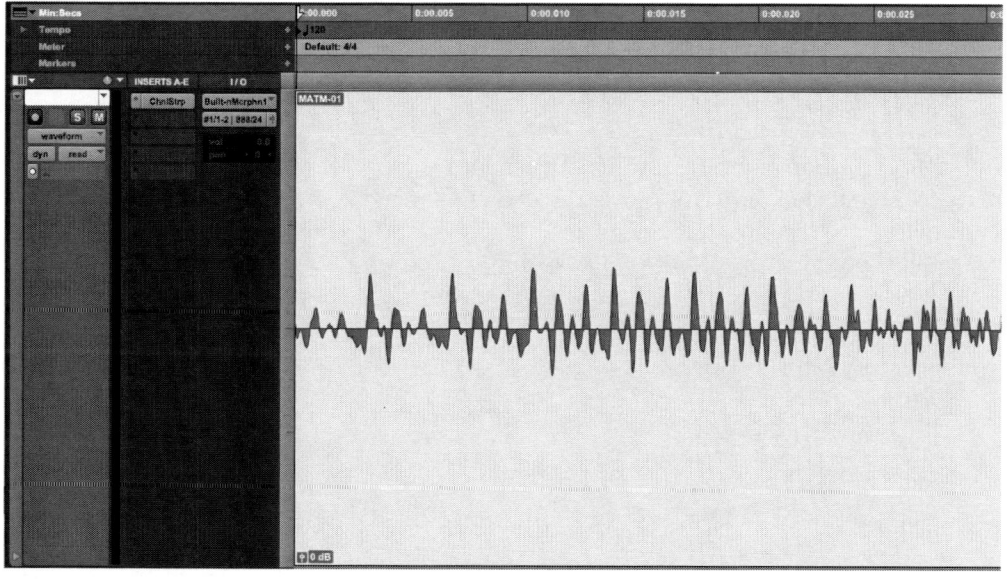

FIGURE 4.9 Linear graph: a typical waveform display

Another type of linear graph in audio might show relative levels. For example, Figure 4.10 shows an audio fundamental and its relative harmonics.

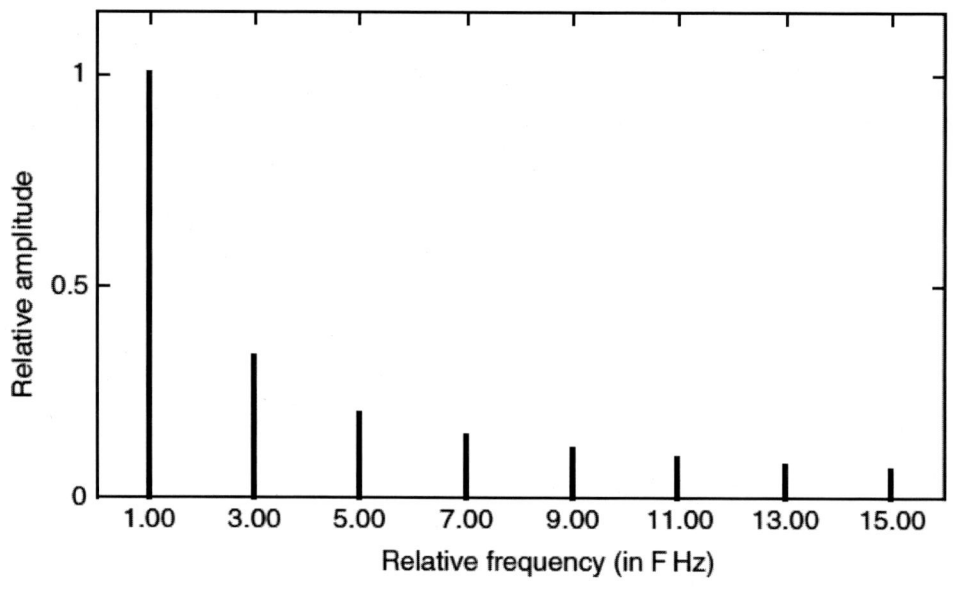

FIGURE 4.10 Linear graph: a fundamental frequency and its harmonics

However, *logarithmic* graphs are useful when dealing with a range of different numbers, from very small to very large. Because we can hear from 20 Hz to 20,000 Hz, you will often see a graph like Figure 4.11, which shows how we can narrow down a scale that would otherwise be 20,000 units long into a smaller, manageable size. This enables us to see the entire range of human hearing on one screen. If one Hertz (Hz) had to fit on each vertical line, we would run out of space!

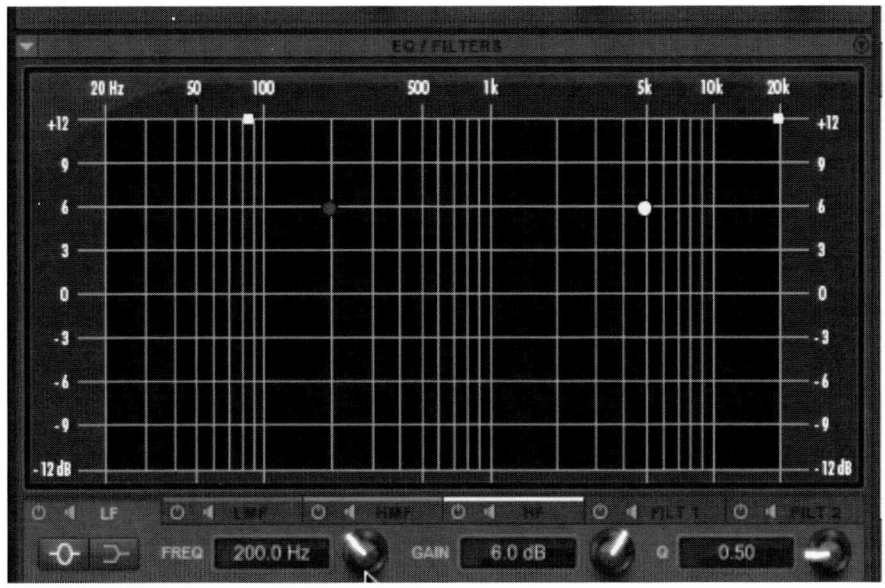

FIGURE 4.11 A logarithmic display used in an EQ

Polar Graphs

A polar graph is useful for showing microphone polar patterns. Suppose we record sound by placing speakers around a mic (Figure 4.12).

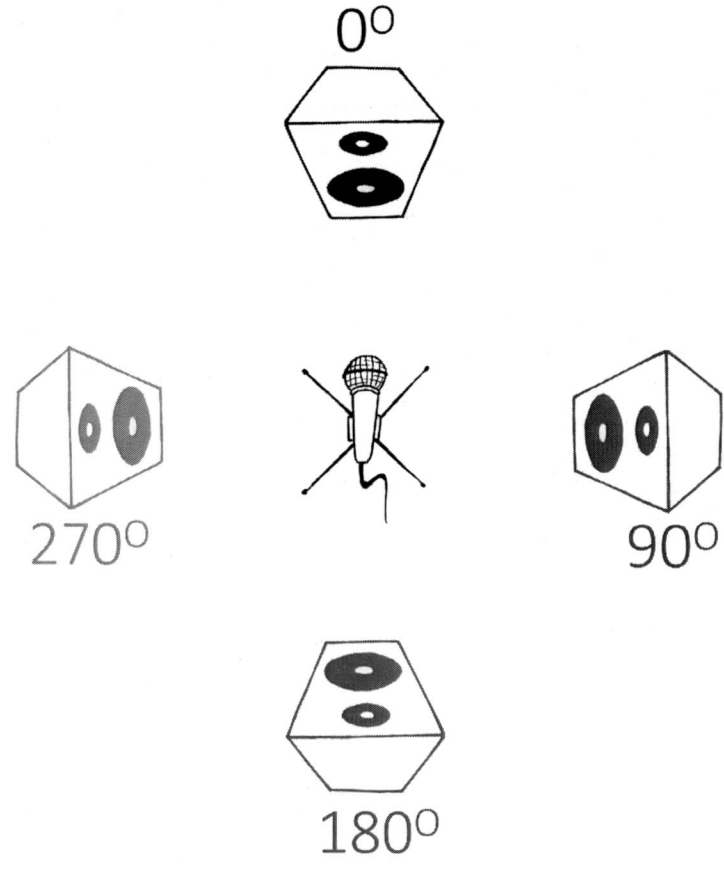

FIGURE 4.12 Speakers placed around a microphone at various angles

In reality, the mic is rotated in front of a speaker in an anechoic chamber but this is just another way to visualize the graph. The frequency response might look like Figure 4.13, which shows 0°, the on-axis position of the mic.

READING GRAPHS 91

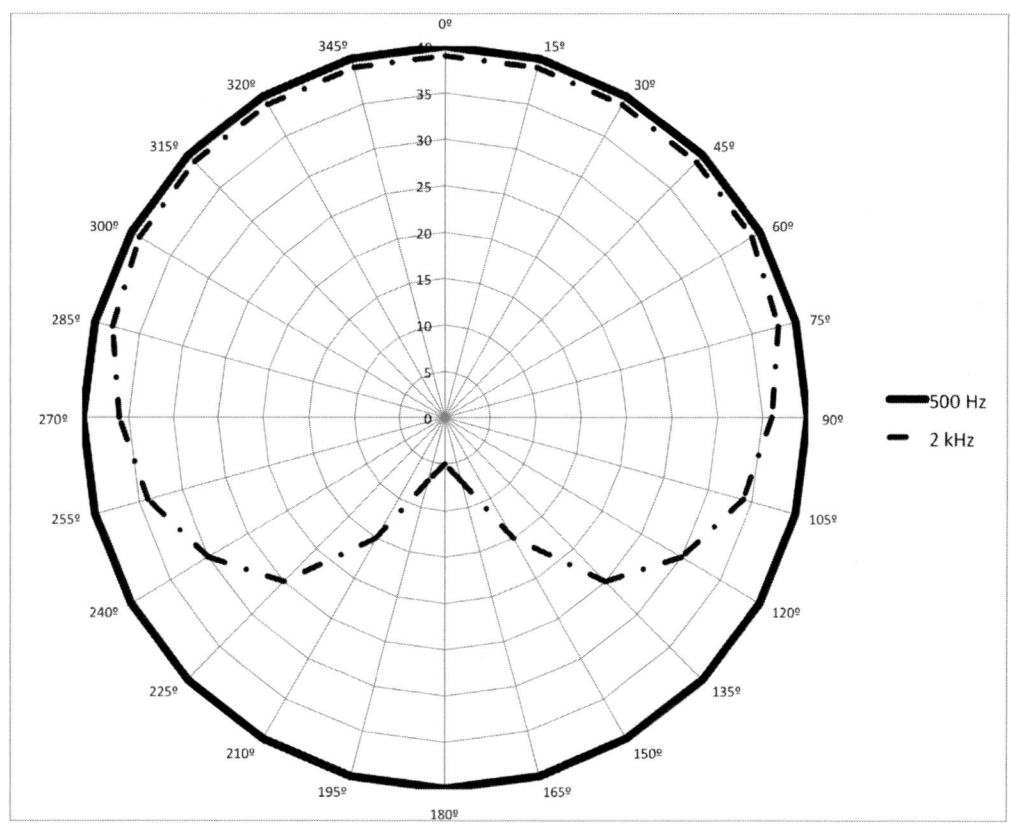

FIGURE 4.13 Polar plot showing 2 different frequency responses of a microphone

Then the frequency response is measured as the microphone is turned 360°. You can see that different frequencies (2 kHz in this example) are a little bit quieter if the sound is coming from the rear of the microphone at 180°. By the way then, that same polar graph would look like Figure 4.14 when plotted on a linear graph.

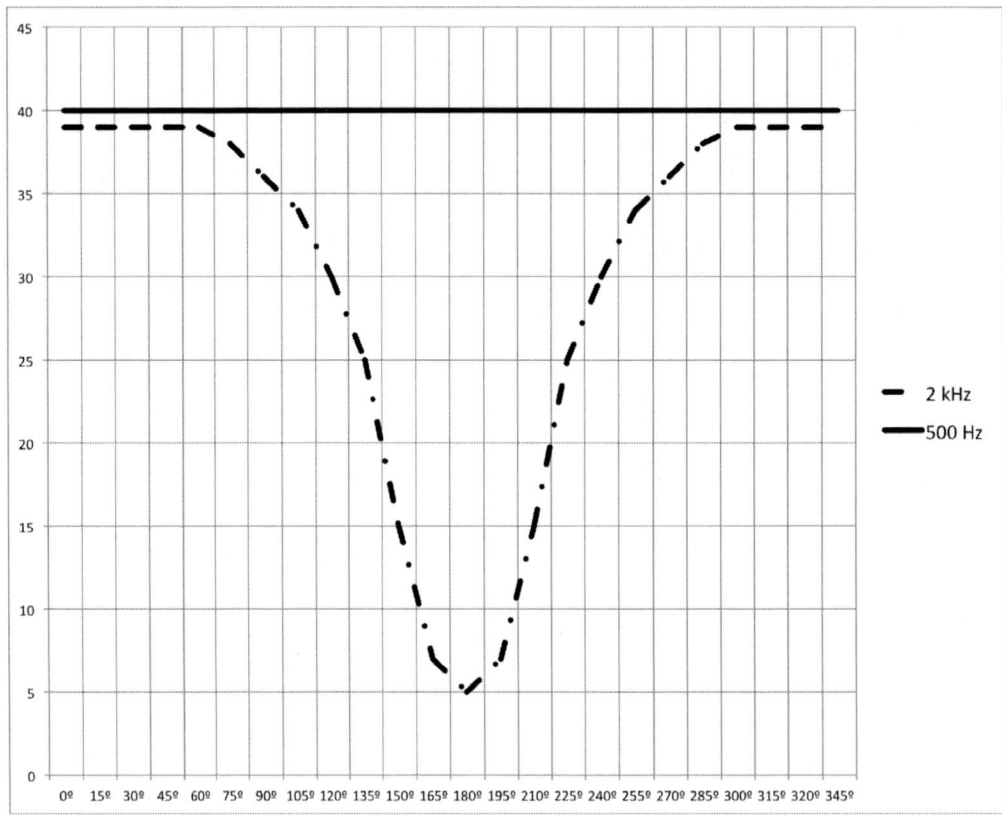

FIGURE 4.14 Linear plot showing 2 different frequency responses of a microphone

FIVE
Audio and Geometry

If you're thinking the only reason you need circles in sound engineering is because of the volume knob (it's round, right?), then think again. And since sound propagates in a sphere, remembering some facts about the geometry of a sphere will be very helpful for you in your audio studies.

GEOMETRY OF A CIRCLE

The geometry of circles has everything to do with sine functions, and sine waves have everything to do with sound. So let's reacquaint ourselves with the geometry of a circle and discover why this is so.

If you play drums, guitar or bass, you often work with the diameter of a circle, as in, "I need a 28-inch bass drum head," or "That speaker cab has 10-inch drivers." Or if you have a subwoofer in your car, it might be 16 inches in diameter.

The circumference of a circle is really important for understanding how the sine function works. The circumference of a circle is $2\pi r$, where r is the radius (Figure 5.1).

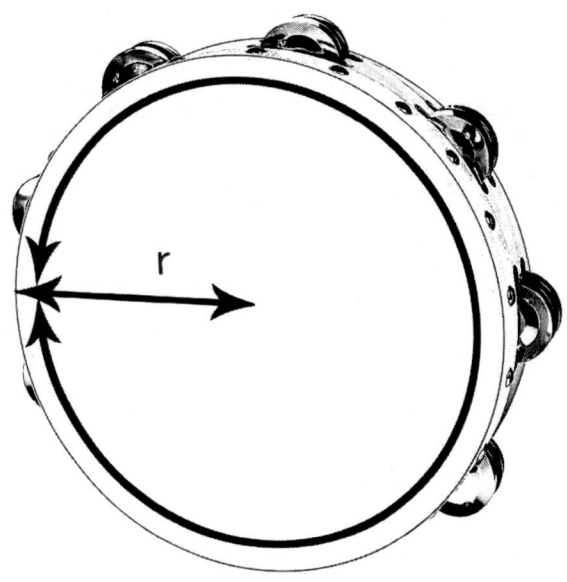

FIGURE 5.1 The radius and circumference of a circle

If the radius of the circle is 4, then the circumference is given by

$$2\pi r = C$$
$$2 \cdot \pi \cdot 4 = C$$
$$3.14 \cdot 8 = 25.13$$

GEOMETRY OF A SPHERE

The surface area of a sphere is $4\pi r^2$. This is quite a handy fact when you realize that sound propagates in a sphere. How can we use this formula for audio? You will read in your text that the intensity of sound drops 6 dB SPL (sound pressure level) for each doubling of distance. To be precise, the number is 6.02 dB SPL—one of our "magic numbers"!

We found a magic number

This number was found by using the surface area of a sphere to compare how sound energy dissipates from one point to the next. Let's take a look.

SOUND PROPAGATION AND INTENSITY: THE INVERSE SQUARE LAW

Recall this formula for finding decibels from chapter 3, p. 000:

$$10 \log \frac{A}{B}$$

And recall how we worked with exponents in equation 3-4:

$$10 \log \frac{4\pi r_1^2}{4\pi r_2^2}$$

$$20 \log \frac{4\pi r_1}{4\pi r_2}$$

$$20 \log \frac{r_1}{r_2}$$

The inverse square law is used in other disciplines besides audio. It describes any relationship where something (in this case, sound intensity) is *inversely proportional* to the square of the distance from the source. This can also work for light or gravity.

Back in the Basic Math Review (p. 8) we saw that the log of 2 is 0.301, one of our magic numbers. Now here is a small twist! If r_2 is twice as far away as r_1, then:

$$20 \log \frac{r_1}{r_2} \, dB$$

$$20 \log \frac{1}{2} \, dB$$

$$20 \log 0.5 \, dB$$

$$20 \cdot -0.301 \, dB$$

But wait ... is that a *negative symbol* in front of our magic number? Yes! Let's continue the equation:

$$20 \cdot -0.301 \, dB$$

$$-6.02 \, dB$$

This negative value is a way of saying that the sound intensity at r_2 is 6 dB *less than* the sound at r_1. This makes sense, because the further away you are from something, the quieter it will be (Figure 5.2).

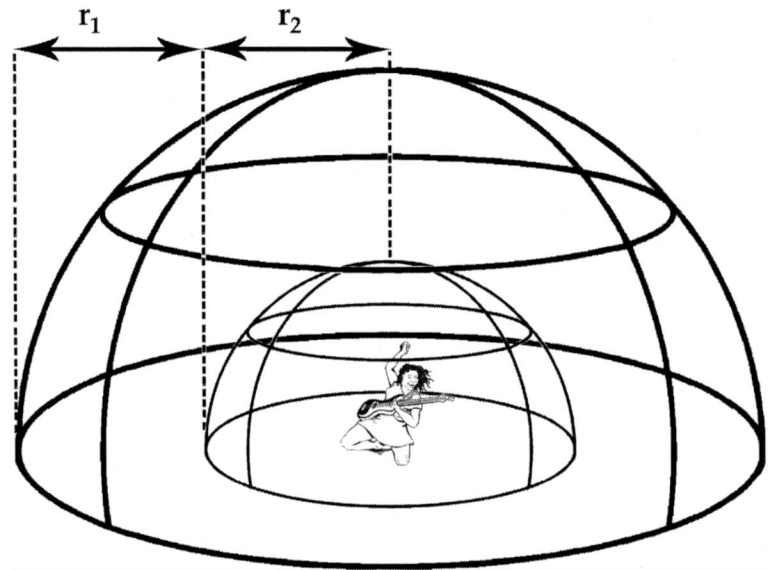

FIGURE 5.2 Sound decreases by 6.02 dB as distance is doubled

WORKING WITH VOLUME

Rooms (such as studios, concert halls, and living rooms) represent three-dimensional spaces where we must take volume into account. Not volume meaning "loudness," but a measurement of space. In order to determine the volume of a rectangular box, you may recall that volume = length × width × height as shown here:

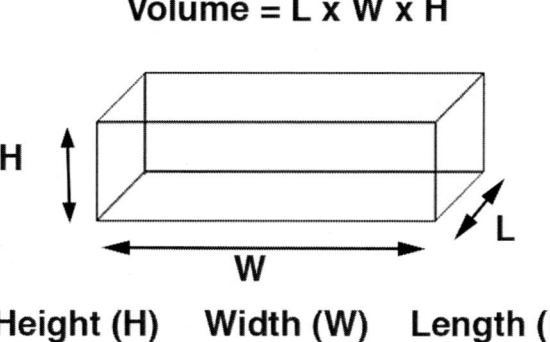

FIGURE 5.3 The volume of a cuboid

In acoustics, determining the volume of a space is done routinely. In order to make a room sound good, acousticians try to manage the sound bouncing off floors, ceilings, and walls by (1) using various absorptive and diffusive materials and (2) making the room large or small enough for its intended purpose.

THE GEOMETRIC MEAN

Why do we use the geometric mean? In chapter 1, we saw a figure of an equalizer with a peak at 200 Hz, a Q of 10, and an indication of where the bandwidth would be.

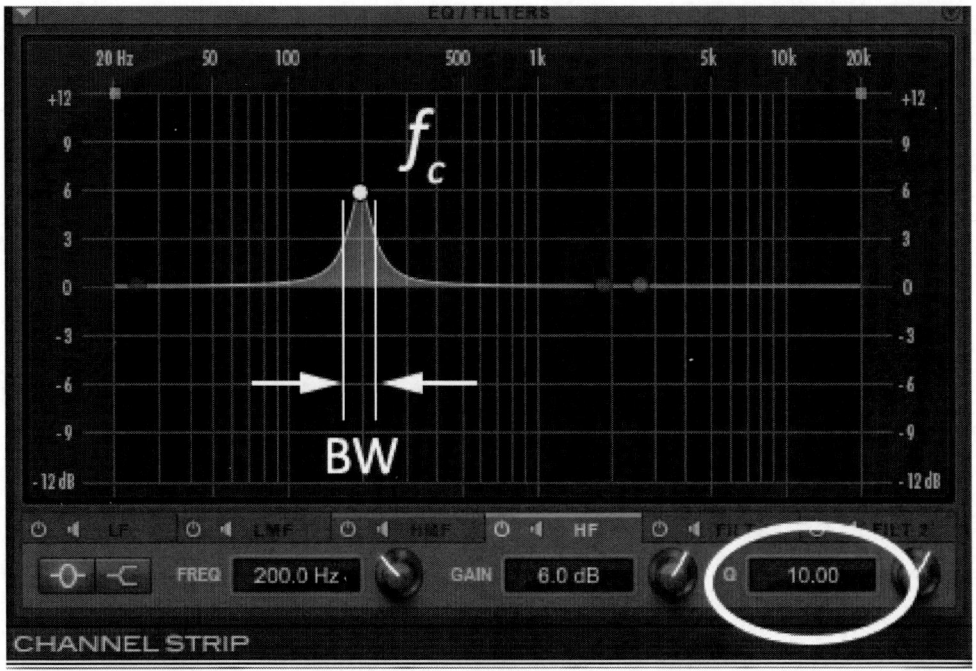

FIGURE 5.4 A peak filter showing an f_c of 200 Hz and a Q of 10

In Figure 5.4 you see a narrow boost at 200 Hz. The Q is 10—a relatively high number in this case—while the bandwidth is very small. The point on the left vertical line that intersects with the 3 dB line is a little below 200 Hz and the point on the right vertical line that intersects at 3 dB is a little above 200 Hz. Using the equation, we can determine from the figure that

$$Q = \frac{f_c}{BW}$$

$$10 = \frac{200\ Hz}{BW}$$

$$BW = \frac{200\ Hz}{10}$$

$$BW = 20\ Hz$$

Now instead of guessing where the end points are ("a little below and above 200Hz"), the bandwidth tells us that there are 20 Hz between the two lines. At first glance, it seems that half of that (10 Hz) is on the left side of the center frequency, and the other half (10 Hz) is on the right side. Thus, it would seem that the bandwidth of 20 Hz spans from 190 Hz (200 – 10 Hz) to 210 Hz (200 + 10 Hz). However, in order to find values for the upper and lower frequencies, we use the *geometric mean*. The value for the lower frequency is actually 190.25 Hz and the upper frequency is 210.25 Hz.

We determined that the bandwidth was 20 Hz, but cautioned that instead of ranging from 190 Hz to 210 Hz, the values were 190.25 and 210.25. Why is this? Consider another example with Figure 5.5 below, which shows two lines, both of which begin at 300 Hz and end at 3,000 Hz.

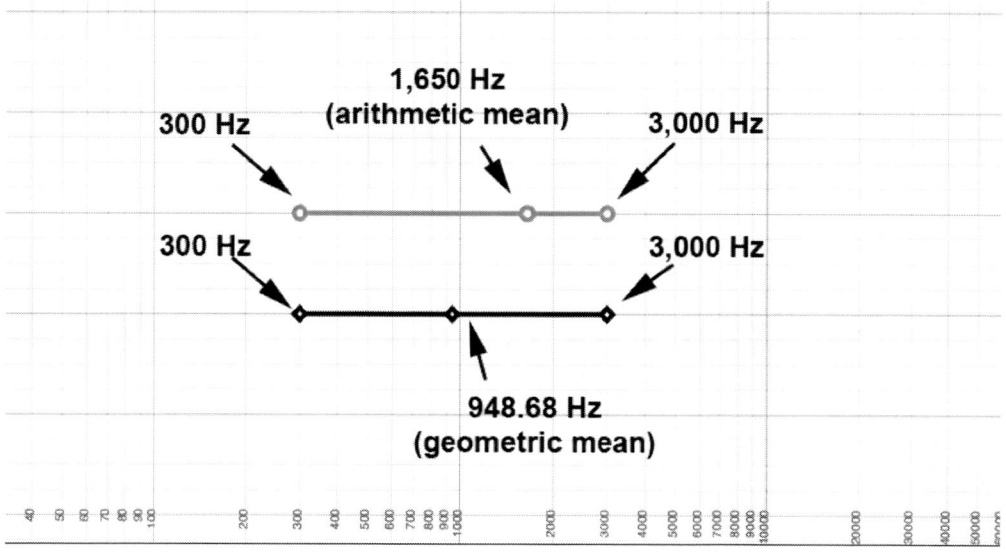

FIGURE 5.5 Arithmetic and geometric means represented on a logarithmic graph

In both cases the bandwidth is 2,700 Hz. However, if we take the *average* of the lowest and highest frequency in order to find the midpoint, we get an answer of 1,650 Hz.

$$f_0 = \frac{f_1 + f_2}{2}$$

$$f_0 = \frac{300 + 3,000}{2}$$

$$f_0 = \frac{3,300}{2}$$

$$f_0 = 1,650$$

As you can see, 1,650 Hz is *not* midway between 300 and 3,000 on the logarithmic graph. Instead, we need to use the geometric mean. If you are using two terms, the expression is:

$$f_0 = \sqrt{f_1 \cdot f_2}$$

$$f_0 = \sqrt{300 \cdot 3{,}000}$$

$$f_0 = \sqrt{900{,}000}$$

$$f_0 = 948.68$$

As shown in the figure, 948.68 lies equidistant between 300 and 3,000 on a logarithmic scale.

More to Know

The geometric mean of two numbers is:

$$\sqrt[2]{x_1 \cdot x_2}$$

The geometric mean of three numbers is:

$$\sqrt[3]{x_1 \cdot x_2 \cdot x_3}$$

The geometric mean of *n* numbers is:

$$\sqrt[n]{x_1 \cdot x_2 \cdot \ldots \cdot x_n}$$

In Figure 5.6, we see a peak filter with a crossover frequency of 3,000 Hz. The Q is given as 2. The crossover frequencies are the points on each side of the curve that are 3 dB lower than the peak level of 6 dB.

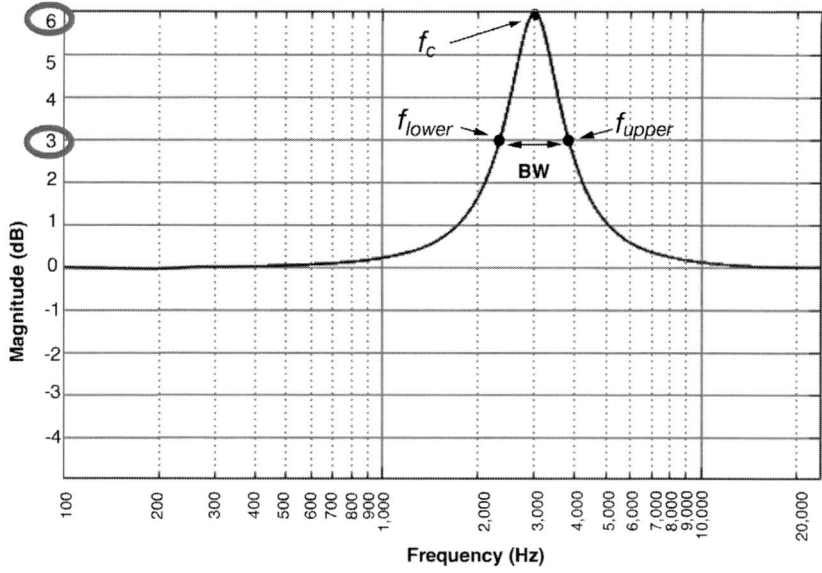

FIGURE 5.6 A peak filter with an f_c of 3,000 Hz and a Q of 2

Given the Q, you can find the bandwidth. Recall from chapter 1 that

$$Q = \frac{f_c}{BW}$$

To find the bandwidth:

$$BW = \frac{f_c}{Q}$$

$$BW = \frac{3{,}000}{2}$$

$$BW = 1{,}500$$

If you know the Q and the bandwidth and would like to determine the upper and lower cutoff (or crossover) frequencies, you would use the following two equations. Recall that simply taking the midpoint of 1,500 (which is 750) will not give us the correct results. For the lower frequency the equation is:

$$f_{lower} = f_c \left(\sqrt{1 + \frac{1}{4Q^2}} - \frac{1}{2Q} \right)$$

For the upper frequency the equation is:

$$f_{lower} = f_c \left(\sqrt{1 + \frac{1}{4Q^2}} - \frac{1}{2Q} \right)$$

With our center frequency of 3,000 and Q of 2, we'll see how to find the lower cutoff frequencies, and then you can try your hand at finding the upper frequency.

$$f_{lower} = f_c \left(\sqrt{1 + \frac{1}{4Q^2}} - \frac{1}{2Q} \right)$$

$$f_{lower} = 3{,}000 \left(\sqrt{1 + \frac{1}{4 \cdot 2^2}} - \frac{1}{2 \cdot 2} \right)$$

$$f_{lower} = 3{,}000 \left(\sqrt{1 + \frac{1}{4 \cdot 4}} - \frac{1}{2 \cdot 2} \right)$$

$$f_{lower} = 3{,}000 \left(\sqrt{1 + \frac{1}{16}} - \frac{1}{4} \right)$$

$$f_{lower} = 3{,}000 \left(\sqrt{1 + 0.0625} - \frac{1}{4} \right)$$

$$f_{lower} = 3{,}000 \left(\sqrt{1.0625} - \frac{1}{4} \right)$$

$$f_{lower} = 3{,}000 \left(1.030776 - \frac{1}{4} \right)$$

$$f_{lower} = 3{,}000 \cdot 0.780776$$

$$f_{lower} = 2342.329$$

Now that we have found the lower frequency, try your hand at finding the upper cutoff frequency:

Exercise 5-1

Given that $fc = 3{,}000$ and $Q = 2$, find the upper cutoff frequency using the equation:

$$f_{upper} = f_c \left(\sqrt{1 + \frac{1}{4Q^2}} + \frac{1}{2Q} \right)$$

SIX
Audio and Trigonometry

From time to time I teach a third-year college-level audio production class. One of my favorite lectures involves showing students the connections between the sine wave, cosine wave, unit circle, and common values used in audio computations.

SINE AND COSINE

We have seen plenty of sine waves in earlier chapters. Let's have a look now at the cosine function (Figure 6.1).

FIGURE 6.1 A way to visualize sine and cosine

Imagine you are at a parade, complete with drums and a majorette twirling a baton. The motion of the baton can be perceived in a few different ways (refer to Figure 6.1):

- If you are in front of the majorette watching the parade head towards you, you would see the baton creating a circular pattern.
- If you are watching from the side (perhaps in a comfy picnic chair with a glass of lemonade), you might see the baton going up and down. The lingering image of the shadow on the side of a building might be a sine wave.
- If you are a mighty eagle flying above the parade, you would see perceive a side-to-side motion of the baton. The lingering image of the shadow on the sidewalk might be a cosine wave.

Note that in each case, the motion of the baton is the same. The only thing that changes is your position relative to the wave.

THE UNIT CIRCLE

The unit circle is analogous to our parade position in front of the majorette. It is a circle with a radius of 1. In Figure 6.2, you can see that each angle corresponds to a unit denoted in radians.

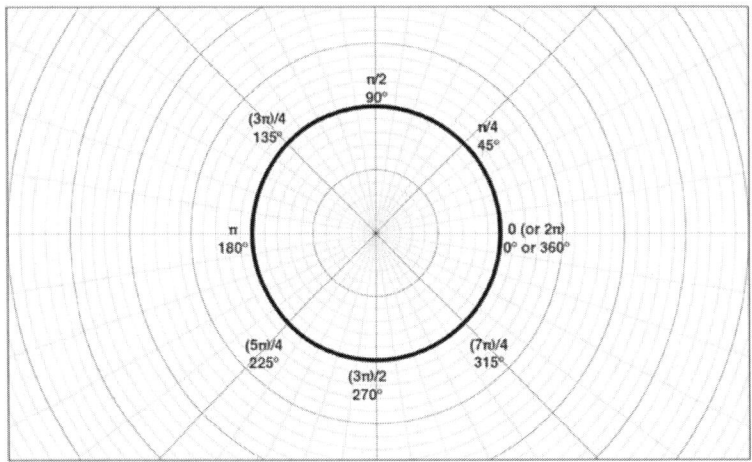

FIGURE 6.2 The unit circle

In more advanced equations, such as those used in Fourier synthesis or calculating inductive and capacitive reactance values and phase, the unit circle can help us think about frequency in a different way, as described in the next section on angular velocity. Each point on the wave can represent a value in radians, which corresponds to the distance travelled by the edge of the baton.

ANGULAR VELOCITY

Let's keep in mind the majorette from the parade in Figure 6.2. This gives us another measurement to consider: radians per second. In other words, the speed of the baton during this time. As you can imagine, as the majorette moves the baton through the air, she is capable of making some complex moves, which cannot be simply described.

Likewise, an audio signal takes a number of twists and turns around the x axis, and it can be useful to describe the speed obtained by the wave in a certain period of time. This is given by the formula

$$\omega = 2\pi f$$

where ω is the lowercase Greek character for "omega." Let's take a look at how this works with a car: perhaps on its way to Milwaukee (Figure 6.3)?

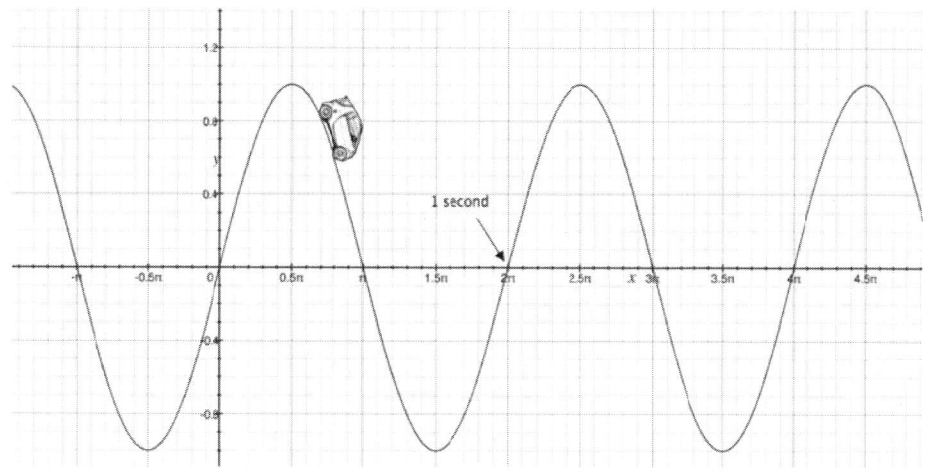

FIGURE 6.3 A car travels along a sine wave

Suppose it takes one second for a cycle to complete. The frequency of the wave is 1 Hz. Now suppose it takes 1 second for *two* cycles to complete.

106 MATH FUNDAMENTALS FOR AUDIO

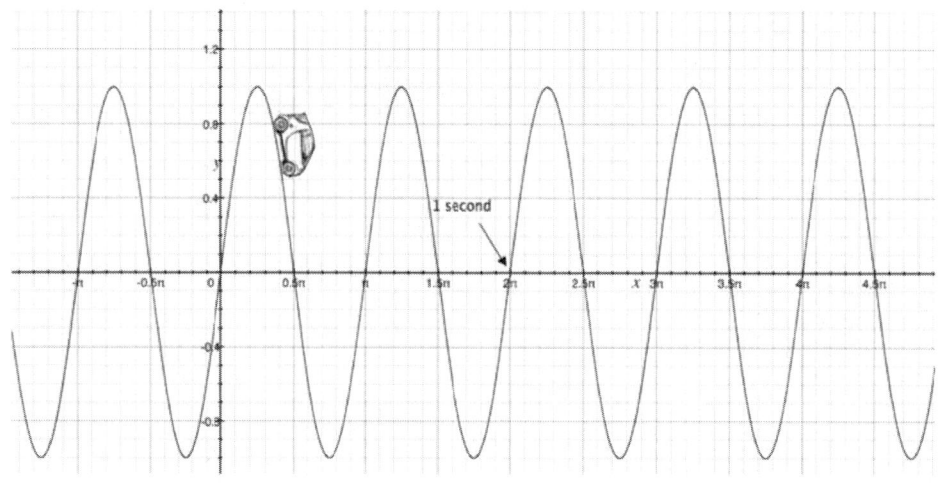

FIGURE 6.4 A sine wave with a frequency of 2 Hz

In Figure 6.4, the frequency of the wave is 2 Hz. Two cycles are completed in one second. So the way to think about angular velocity is, *What is the speed of the car when the frequency is 2 Hz?*

$$\omega = 2\pi f$$

$$\omega = 2\pi(2)\frac{rad}{s}$$

$$\omega = 4\pi \text{ rad/s}$$

$$\omega = 12.56\frac{rad}{s}$$

The angular velocity of the car is 12.56 radians per second. It makes sense that if the frequency is slower, the car will take longer to get to its destination.

More to Know

In order to convert Cartesian coordinates to polar coordinates, recall some trigonometric functions. If you have the coordinates (x,y), you can find "r" with the Pythagorean theorem.

$$r = \sqrt{x^2 + y^2}$$

Equation 6-1: Finding angle using Cartesian coordinates

In Figure 6.5, x = 3 and y = 2, therefore

$$r = \sqrt{3^2 + 2^2}$$
$$r = \sqrt{9 + 4}$$
$$r = \sqrt{13}$$
$$r = 3.606$$

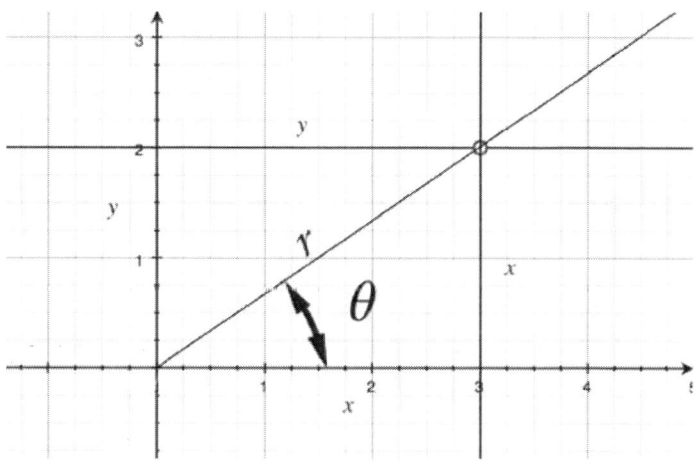

FIGURE 6.5 Finding the radius using Cartesian coordinates

Similarly, you can find θ by using a trigonometric equation:

$$\tan \theta = \frac{x}{y}$$

$$\tan \theta = \frac{3}{2}$$

$$\tan \theta = 1.5$$

In order to find θ, you need a calculator that can perform the "arctan" function

$$\arctan 1.5 = 56.310º$$

SEVEN
Audio and Calculus

So far, this book has introduced some relatively basic concepts. Yet many more mathematical applications in audio cover such concepts as imaginary numbers, phase shift, vector math, and more. In this chapter, I simply ask that you observe how to derive a very simple equation. You may or may not have had calculus, but in my research I have not uncovered any other texts that describe this process, and I thought you might benefit from it—or at least find it interesting. With that in mind, let's begin by looking at a familiar audio term RMS.

RMS

RMS stands for "root-mean-squared," the square *root* of the *mean* (average) of all *squared* values taken at equal intervals on a waveform (Figure 7.1).

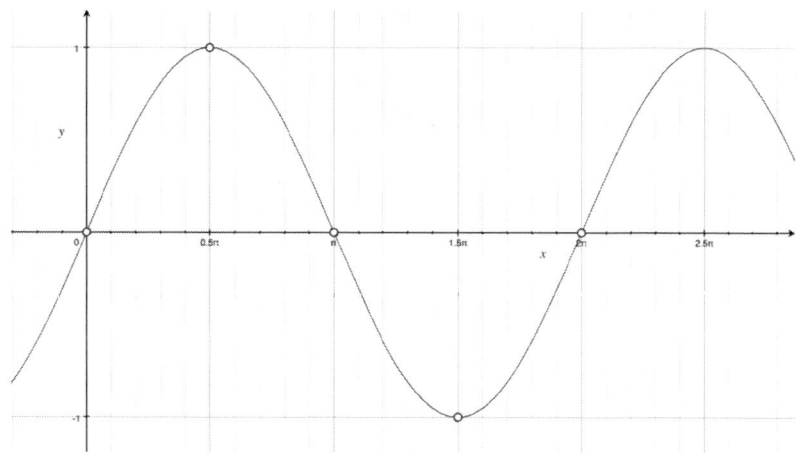

FIGURE 7.1 Sine wave with points highlighted at $\pi/2$, π, $3\pi/2$, and 2π

$$y = \sqrt{\frac{(\sin\frac{\pi}{2})^2 + (\sin\pi)^2 + (\sin\frac{3\pi}{2})^2 + (\sin 2\pi)^2}{4}}$$

$$y = \sqrt{\frac{(\sin(1))^2 + (\sin(0))^2 + (\sin(-1))^2 + (\sin(0))^2}{4}}$$

$$y = \sqrt{\frac{2}{4}}$$

$$y = .707$$

We found a magic number: 0.707

This can also be written as

$$rms = \frac{peak}{\sqrt{2}}$$

or, since $\frac{1}{\sqrt{2}} = 0.707$,

$$rms = peak \cdot 0.707$$

The square root of 2 is 1.414. So if the peak value is 1:

$$rms = \frac{1}{\sqrt{2}}$$

$$rms = \frac{1}{1.414}$$

$$rms = 0.707$$

As a matter of fact, RMS is often given as:

$$rms = 0.707 \times peak$$

DERIVING SIGNAL-TO-NOISE RATIO OF A PCM SYSTEM

An Advanced Look at Signal-to-Noise Ratio

Many textbooks say that you can determine the resolution of a digital audio (PCM) system by multiplying the number of bits by 6. So, a 16-bit session would have a signal-to-noise ratio of 96 dB. But is it really 6 dB per bit? More advanced textbooks will go further and describe the resolution of a system as

$$6.02n + 1.76$$

where n is the number of bits. It is important to keep in mind throughout this exercise that this only works with perfect sine waves, and audio signals are of course more complex.

Deriving the signal-to-noise ratio (or "signal-to-error ratio"—in a digital system, errors are perceived as noise, as we'll explain) is a good practice, but it's not very easy to solve. In this section, we'll see how it's done.

The infamous "$6.02n + 1.76$" figure is an RMS measurement. We determined in equation 7-1 that in order to find an RMS value, we divide the peak value by the square root of 2. This is written as

$$rms = \frac{peak}{\sqrt{2}}$$

To set up the signal-to-error formula, let's examine the terms "signal" and "error" more closely.

The Signal

The signal is measured by the number of quantization levels available in the system, and is given by 2^n. For example, in a 16-bit system, there are 2^{16} (or 65,536) places where a bit number is assigned to the signal's voltage. In a 24-bit system, there are 2^{24} (or 16,777,216) such places. Perhaps you can see already that a 24-bit system will be more accurate—meaning less error.

In Figure 7.3, we are using a 3-bit system with 8 quantization steps. The peak value of the signal is actually the number from the zero axis to the peak of the system. This value is divided by two, since we're only using the top half of the wave. In other words,

$$\frac{2^n}{2}$$

The size of each interval is $1/2^n$, and the graph is made up of 2^n levels. Each interval is $1/2^n$ tall. Here's another way to think about it: In a 3-bit system, 2^n would be 2^3 (and $2^3 = 8$). In this system, there would be eight levels altogether. Each level would be 1/8 units high or $1/2^3$ units high. The peak would be 4 units high (Figure 7.2).

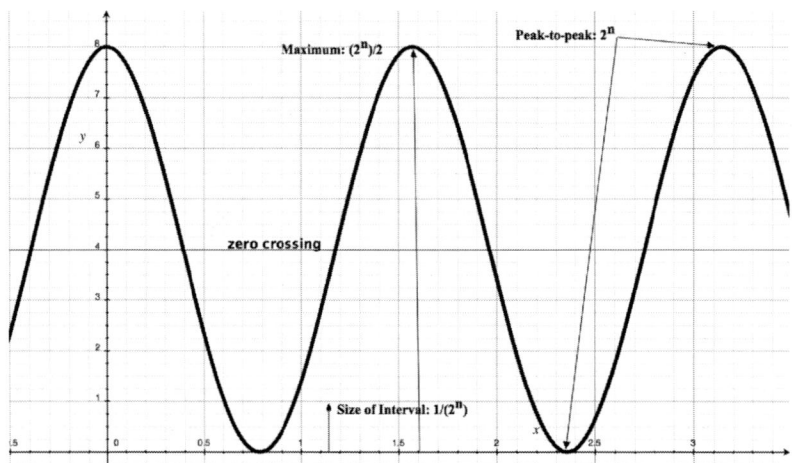

FIGURE 7.2 Viewing quantization levels on a 3-bit scale

Thus, the peak is the maximum value divided by two and multiplied by the size of each of interval, or

$$\frac{2^n}{2} \cdot \frac{1}{2^n}$$

Given that $\frac{1}{2\sqrt{2}}$ (where $b = \sqrt{2}$), the RMS value of this number would be:

$$\frac{2^n}{2} \cdot \frac{1}{2^n} \cdot \frac{1}{\sqrt{2}}$$

$$\frac{\cancel{2^n}}{2} \cdot \frac{1}{\cancel{2^n}} \cdot \frac{1}{\sqrt{2}}$$

or

$$\frac{1}{2\sqrt{2}}$$

Thus, the number used for the RMS value of the signal is $\frac{1}{2\sqrt{2}}$.

The Error

The number for error is more difficult to derive and involves calculus and a "probability density function" (pdf). Consider that within two intervals, there is a certain probability that the number chosen will be either right or wrong (Figure 7.3).

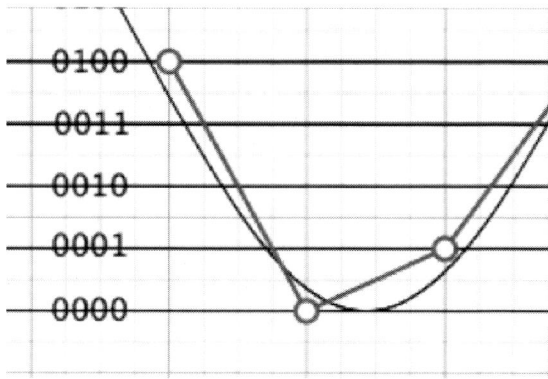

FIGURE 7.3 A 4-bit system showing errors in aligning with the original waveform

In this four-bit system, there is a great chance that the chosen value will be wrong. Notice in Figure 7.4 how the circles where bit values are assigned do not line up precisely with the waveform. Thus a four-bit system has a low signal-to-error ratio (6.02(4) + 1.076 = 25.15 dB!). This will sound very noisy and quite terrible!

Error and Probability Density Function

The error is based on the probability that the right or wrong bit value will be assigned. There is a given formula for the probability density function:

$$\sqrt{\int_{-\infty}^{\infty} e^2 p(e) de}$$

Rather than explore the equation for probability density function in detail, let's just assume that someone else has done the hard work of figuring out how likely it is that a digital system will "pick the right number" and use it as a basis for setting up the problem.

In a digital audio system, each quantization interval is Q, where Q is the size of a quantization interval (also written as $1/2^n$). And instead of $\pm\infty$, the limits change to be the top and bottom of an interval, or $\pm Q/2$:

$$\sqrt{\frac{1}{Q}\int_{-\frac{Q}{2}}^{\frac{Q}{2}} e^2 \, de}$$

Just as we learned some ways to simplify logarithm expressions in chapter 3, you can do the same with integration formulas. Here's one example.

$$\int x^n \, dx$$

can be written as

$$\frac{x^{n+1}}{n+1}$$

so if we substitute x^n for $(q/2)^2$:

$$\frac{x^{n+1}}{n+1}$$

$$\frac{\frac{q^{2+1}}{2}}{2+1}$$

$$\frac{\frac{q^3}{2}}{3}$$

Also,

$$\int_a^b f(x) \, dx$$

can be written as Figure 7.4.

$$F(x) \Big|_a^b$$

FIGURE 7.4 Integration line

This can be expressed as

$$F(b) - F(a)$$

$$\int_a^b f(x)\,dx = F(x)\Big|_a^b = F(b) - F(a).$$

Substituting $Q/2$ for e:

$$\sqrt{\frac{1}{Q}\cdot\frac{\left(\frac{Q}{2}\right)^3}{3}-\frac{1}{Q}\cdot\frac{\left(-\frac{Q}{2}\right)^3}{3}}$$

$$\sqrt{\frac{1}{Q}\cdot\frac{(Q)^3}{2^3\cdot 3}-\frac{1}{Q}\cdot\frac{(-Q)^3}{2^3\cdot 3}}$$

$$\sqrt{\frac{1}{Q}\cdot\frac{(Q)^3}{8\cdot 3}-\frac{1}{Q}\cdot\frac{(-Q)^3}{8\cdot 3}}$$

(Q^3/Q) becomes Q^2:

$$\sqrt{\frac{1}{\cancel{Q}}\cdot\frac{\cancel{(Q)^3}}{8\cdot 3}-\frac{1}{\cancel{Q}}\cdot\frac{\cancel{(Q)^3}}{8\cdot 3}}$$

$$\sqrt{\frac{Q^2}{24}+\frac{Q^2}{24}}$$

$$\sqrt{\frac{2Q^2}{24}}$$

$$\sqrt{\frac{Q^2}{12}}$$

$$\frac{\sqrt{Q^2}}{\sqrt{12}}$$

$$\frac{Q}{\sqrt{12}}$$

Or, since $Q = 1/2^n$

$$\frac{1}{2^n}\times\frac{1}{\sqrt{12}}$$

Therefore, the error is equal to

$$E = \frac{1}{2^n\sqrt{12}}$$

Signal to Error

So, the signal-to-error ratio has the signal in the numerator, which we found to be:

$$\frac{1}{2\sqrt{2}}$$

and the error in the denominator, which we found to be:

$$\frac{1}{2^n\sqrt{12}}$$

Therefore, we set up the ratio as the signal divided by the error:

$$\frac{1}{2\sqrt{2}} \div \frac{1}{2^n\sqrt{12}}$$

or multiply by the reciprocal:

$$\frac{1}{2\sqrt{2}} \cdot \frac{2^n\sqrt{12}}{1}$$

and the signal to error ratio can be expressed as

$$\frac{2^n\sqrt{12}}{2\sqrt{2}}$$

Finally, to describe the signal to error ratio in decibels, the logarithm of this ratio is squared and multiplied by 10.

$$\frac{S}{E} = 10 \log \left(\frac{2^n\sqrt{12}}{2\sqrt{2}}\right)^2$$

Each term in brackets can be squared:

$$\frac{S}{E} = 10\log\left(\frac{2^{2n} \cdot 12}{4 \cdot 2}\right)$$

The 12 in the numerator can be reduced by the 4 in the denominator and becomes 3 in the numerator (12 divided by 4 is 3):

$$\frac{S}{E} = 10\log\left(\frac{2^{2n} \cdot \cancel{12}}{\cancel{4} \cdot 2}\right)$$

$$\frac{S}{E} = 10\log\left(\frac{2^{2n} \cdot 3}{2}\right)$$

Back in chapter 3 (p. 67–80), we learned that

$$logA \cdot logB = logA + logB$$

So we can separate the term above in brackets to 3/2 and 2^{2n}, like this:

$$\frac{S}{E} = 10\log 2^{2n} + 10\log \frac{3}{2}$$

We also learned in chapter 3 that

$$\log A \div \log B = \log A - \log B$$

or in our case:

$$\frac{S}{E} = 10\log 2^{2n} + 10\log 3 - 10\log 2$$

Then, go back to chapter 3 and review:

$$\log A^x = x \cdot \log A$$

Then the equation becomes

$$\frac{S}{E} = 2n \cdot 10\log 2 + 10\log 3 - 10\log 2$$

$$\frac{S}{E} = 20n \cdot \log 2 + 10\log 3 - 10\log 2$$

We can now solve the above terms:

$$\log 2 = .301$$

$$\log 3 = .477$$

$$\frac{S}{E} = (20n \cdot 0.301) + (10 \cdot 0.477) - (10 \cdot .301)$$

$$\frac{S}{E} = (6.02n) + 4.77 - 3.01$$

$$\frac{S}{E} = 6.02n + 1.76$$

or about 6 dB per bit!

EIGHT
The Fourier Transform
by Jamie Angus-Whiteoak

Many of the concepts covered in this book culminate in this chapter on the Fourier Transform (127–27).

FOURIER'S THEOREM

Jean-Baptiste Joseph Fourier (1768–1830) worked on a mathematical model of heat transfer in solid bodies (among many other topics). His thesis *On the Propagation of Heat in Solid Bodies* (1807)[1] contained a novel idea for expanding a continuous function as a sum of sine and cosine waves of different frequencies. In principle, any possible waveform can be broken down into individual sine and cosine components, although sometimes it can take a very large number of them.

Although Fourier developed this as a part of his model for heat transfer, it has a much wider application. Fourier's Theorem is now usually stated as:

> *Any periodic function can be represented as an infinite sum of harmonic sinusoids multiplied by appropriate coefficients.*

Mathematically, this is expressed as

$$f(t) = a_0 + \sum_{n=1}^{\infty} a_n \cos(n\omega_0 t) + b_n \sin(n\omega_0 t)$$

where: $f(t)$ = the periodic time function to be represented
n = the harmonic number
ω_0 = the angular frequency ($2\pi f_0$) of the periodic function
a_0 = the d.c. content of the periodic function
a_n = the level of the nth cosign harmonic of the periodic function
b_n = the level of the nth sine harmonic of the periodic function

The Σ in the equation is the Greek capital letter "S," or "Sigma," which means "sum (add) all the results together, and the number on the bottom indicates where you start the sum and the number on the top is where you finish the sum." This is similar to the limits on an integral.

The periodic function *f(t)* has a period T_0 such that its angular frequency, in radians per second, is given by the equation

$$\omega = \frac{2\pi}{T_0}$$

This is similar to the equation for velocity (p. 105), in which

$$\omega = 2\pi f$$

and equation on the relationship between time and frequency (p. 44), in which

$$T = \frac{1}{f}$$

The sum of the sines and cosines on the right hand side of equation 8-1 is called a Fourier series. The sinusoids are harmonic. This means that all their frequencies are integer multiples of the lowest, or fundamental, frequency ω_0.

The equation at the top of the page states that, provided we know the correct values for the amplitudes of the sinusoids a_n and b_n, we can add them up make any periodic signal *f(t)* we like. Different signals will need different values for a_n and b_n. The act of summing the harmonic sinusoids together to make a signal is called Fourier synthesis. This is just like using additive synthesis to generate a particular waveform or sound on a synthesizer. Let's see how this works.

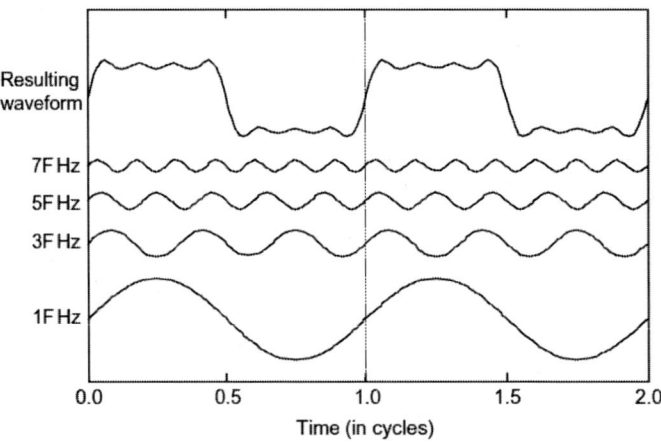

FIGURE 8.1 The effect of adding four harmonically related sine waves together

Figure 8.1 shows four sine waves whose frequencies are 1F Hz, 3F Hz, 5F Hz, and 7F Hz, and whose amplitude is inversely proportional to the frequency. This means that the 3F Hz component is 1/3 the amplitude of the component at 1F Hz, and so on. When these sine waves are added together, as shown in Figure 8.1, the result approximates a square wave. Figure 8.1 also shows the effect of not having enough coefficients.

To get a better square wave, more high-frequency components must be added. The higher-frequency components are needed in order to provide the fast rise and sharp corners of the square wave. In general, as the rise time gets faster and the corners get sharper, more high-frequency sine waves are required to represent the waveform accurately. We would need an infinite amount to have something that really looked like a square wave!

For the square wave shown in Figure 8.1, the Fourier series coefficients are:

$$a_0 = 0$$

$$a_n = 0$$

$$b_n = \begin{cases} 0, if\ n\ is\ even \\ \dfrac{4}{n\pi}, if n\ is\ odd \end{cases}$$

You will notice that only the sine coefficients b_n are used to make a square wave. What would happen if we had exactly the same frequencies and amplitudes but used cosine waves instead? The result is shown in Figure 8.2.

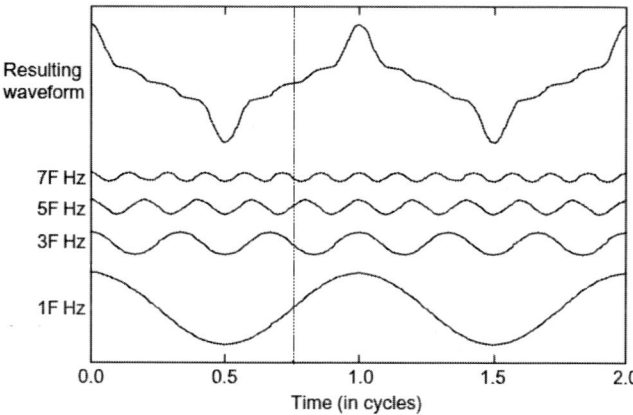

FIGURE 8.2 The effect of adding four harmonically related cosine waves together.

Now we have a completely different waveform—a triangle wave—and just like the square wave, if we added more harmonics together we would get a better approximation to the triangle wave that would be sharper and more pointed.

So what does this mean? It means that for the Fourier series, phase matters! Having the wrong phase means we will get the wrong waveform. So in general we have to use both sine and cosine components to create the desired waveform.

FREQUENCY SPECTRUM

Sometimes we are more interested in magnitudes of the different harmonics that are in the waveform, irrespective of their phases. Plotting the magnitude of the coefficients of the Fourier series gives us its frequency spectrum. This is shown in Figure 8.3.

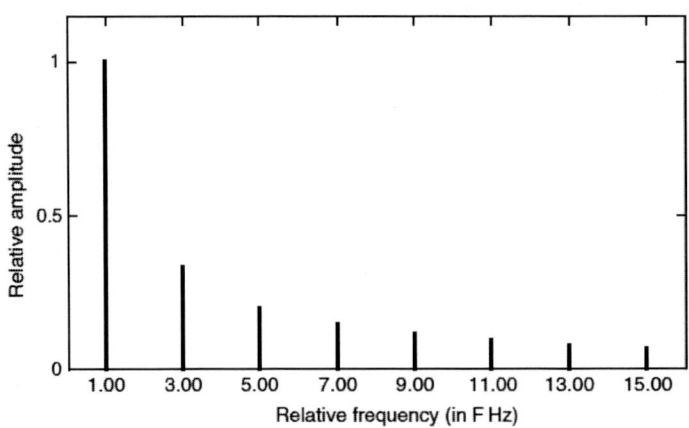

FIGURE 8.3 The frequency spectrum of the waveforms shown in Figures 8.1 and 8.2

The frequency spectrum tells us how much energy the signal has at any particular harmonic, and it often relates to how that waveform will sound. We can convert Figure 8.3 to a real frequency in Hz simply by multiplying each value of relative frequency (F) by the fundamental frequency (f_0).

We can see that the square wave has a lot of energy at the fundamental frequency ($F = 1$). But the amplitude of the other harmonics decreases quite slowly with frequency. In fact, the harmonic amplitude decreases as $1/F$. This slow decay rate is closely associated with the way the square wave looks and how it sounds. A spectrum that falls off as $1/F$ is always associated with a signal with a discontinuity, and if it's periodic, it will sound buzzy.

To get the magnitude of the Fourier coefficients we must combine the values of both the sine and cosine components, as shown in equation 8-4.

$$|C_n| = \frac{\sqrt{a_n^2 + b_n^2}}{2}$$

FOURIER ANALYSIS

The Fourier coefficients discussed earlier are not found by trial and error. Fourier also developed equations for extracting them. For any periodic function $f(t)$ the harmonic coefficients a_0, a_n and b_n can be found as follows.

The dc value (a_0) refers to the steady, nonmodulating version of the signal (a flat line). It occurs when the frequency = 0 and can be found using this equation:

$$a_0 = \frac{1}{T_0} \int_{-\frac{T_0}{2}}^{\frac{T_0}{2}} f(t)\,dt$$

Like the Greek Σ, The $\int$ symbol means "add everything up"; in fact, the symbol is a stylized Elizabethan "S," and the variables at the bottom and top indicate where you start and stop respectively. So what this equation is saying is: add up all the values over one cycle of the waveform and divide it by the length of the waveform. That is, find out the average value of the waveform, which is its dc value.

For the other coefficients, we have to find out how much of the relevant harmonic, both sine and cosine, is in the waveform. We do this by first multiplying the waveform by the relevant harmonic before we find the average value, as shown in equations 8-6 and 8-7.

$$a_n = \frac{2}{T_0} \int_{-\frac{T_0}{2}}^{\frac{T_0}{2}} f(t)\cos(n\omega_0 t)\,dt$$

$$b_n = \frac{2}{T_0} \int_{-\frac{T_0}{2}}^{\frac{T_0}{2}} f(t)\sin(n\omega_0 t)\,dt$$

Using these three equations (a_0 [the dc value], a_n, and b_n) we can find out the harmonic content of any waveform you like. However, the math can get a bit complicated!

FREQUENCY ANALYSIS OF NONPERIODIC SIGNALS: THE FOURIER TRANSFORM

The Fourier series is useful for analyzing periodic signals. However, many signals are nonperiodic—that is, they occur only once. An example would be a single drum beat. This requires a different approach.

We can consider a single instance of a waveform as being like a periodic signal except that the period is infinity—that is,

$$-\frac{T_0}{2} = -\infty$$

and

$$\frac{T_0}{2} = \infty$$

This means that instead of having a series of coefficients, we end up with an equation that describes how the values of the different sine and cosine waves vary with frequency. If we do this, then it possible to come up with a single equation that calculates the following functions:

$$F_a(\omega) = \int_{-\infty}^{\infty} f(t)\cos(\omega t)\,dt$$

$$F_b(\omega) = \int_{-\infty}^{\infty} f(t)\sin(\omega t)\,dt$$

These equations are each known as the Fourier Transform of the function $f(t)$. Note that:

- $F(\omega)$ replaces with a continuous function of angular frequency ω.
- The limits of the integral are now theoretically infinite; however, in practice the integral only has to be calculated over the time range that the signal $f(t)$ is nonzero.
- As matter of convention, time-domain signals are represented using lower case letters, whereas the frequency domain signals use capitals.

Those equations transform the time domain representation of the signal $f(t)$ into the frequency domain representation of the signal $F(\omega)$ that contains both sine and cosine components.

There is a complementary transform that reverses the process and converts the function from the frequency domain back into the time domain:

$$f(t) = \frac{1}{2\pi}\int_{-\infty}^{\infty}\left[F_a(\omega)\cos(\omega t) + F_a(\omega)\sin(\omega t)\right]d\omega$$

The previous two equations, along with the equation above, are known as the "Fourier transform pair" and can be used on any type of signal, whether periodic or nonperiodic. Together, they form a particularly powerful basis for analyzing and processing signals, because it is easier to think about filtering in the frequency domain than the time domain.

A FOURIER TRANSFORM EXAMPLE: THE SINGLE PULSE

Let's do an example to see how this works.

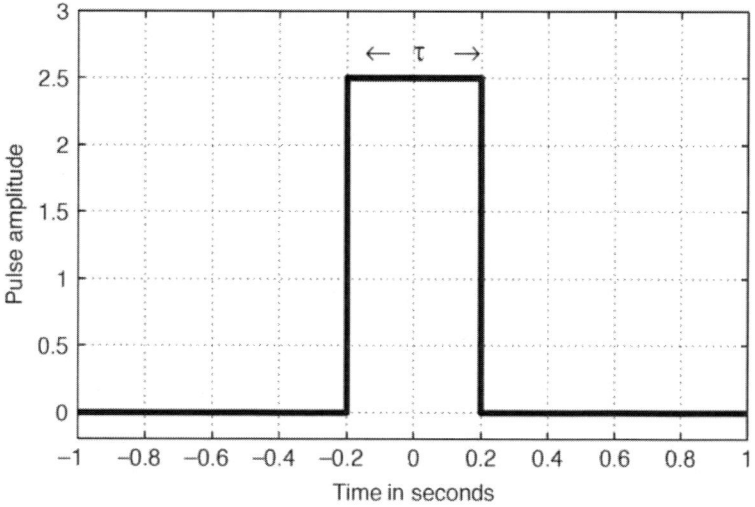

FIGURE 8.4 A single rectangular pulse of length τ and amplitude of $\frac{1}{\tau}$

Figure 8.4 shows a single rectangular pulse of length τ (Tau) seconds and amplitude of $\frac{1}{\tau}$, which is defined mathematically in the equation at the top of this page. Note that, regardless of the value of τ, the area of the pulse is constant and equal to one.

$$f(t) = \begin{cases} \frac{1}{\tau}, & \frac{-\tau}{2} < t < \frac{\tau}{2} \\ 0, & elsewhere \end{cases}$$

To find the Fourier transform of this we need to use the equation at the top of p. 125, as $f(t)$ in the Fourier transform pair equations. Fortunately, this function is zero over most of the range, as the integral of zero is zero. This is because adding lots of zeros together still gives you zero and results in solvable definite integrals with limits $\pm\frac{\tau}{2}$. This is shown in the following equations.

$$F_a(\omega) = \int_{-\frac{\tau}{2}}^{\frac{\tau}{2}} \frac{1}{\tau} \cos(\omega t) dt$$

$$F_b(\omega) = \int_{-\frac{\tau}{2}}^{\frac{\tau}{2}} \frac{1}{\tau} \sin(\omega t) dt$$

Let's look at the second term $F_b(\omega)$ first. Using the rules of integration, the integral of $\sin(x) = -\cos(x)$. This yields the next equation, which, after evaluating the limits, becomes a further equation.

$$F_b(\omega) = \frac{1}{\tau}\left[\frac{-\cos(\omega t)}{\omega}\right]_{-\frac{\tau}{2}}^{\frac{\tau}{2}}$$

$$F_b(\omega) = \frac{-1}{\omega\tau}\left(\cos\left(\omega\frac{\tau}{2}\right) - \cos\left(-\omega\frac{\tau}{2}\right)\right)$$

Now $\cos(x) = \cos(-x)$, so these terms cancel each other out. This is because the pulse is symmetric around $t = 0$.

$$F_b(\omega) = 0$$

Now let's look at the $F_b(\omega)$ term. Using the rules of integration, the integral of $\cos(x) = \sin(x)$

$$F_a(\omega) = \frac{1}{\tau}\left[\frac{\sin(\omega t)}{\omega}\right]_{-\frac{\tau}{2}}^{\frac{\tau}{2}}$$

which, after evaluating the limits becomes

$$F_a(\omega) = \frac{1}{\omega\tau}\left(\sin\left(\omega\frac{\tau}{2}\right) - \sin\left(-\omega\frac{\tau}{2}\right)\right)$$

Now $\sin(-x) = -\sin(x)$, so this equation becomes

$$F_a(\omega) = \frac{1}{\omega\tau}\left(\sin\left(\omega\frac{\tau}{2}\right) + \sin\left(\omega\frac{\tau}{2}\right)\right)$$

which simplifies to

$$F(\omega) = \frac{2}{\omega\tau}\sin\left(\frac{\omega\tau}{2}\right)$$

This can be expressed as:

$$F(\omega) = \frac{\sin\left(\frac{\omega\tau}{2}\right)}{\left(\frac{\omega\tau}{2}\right)}$$

We found a magic number

The function $\frac{\sin(x)}{x}$ is a magic number because it appears so often that it has its own name: sinc(x). So we can say the Fourier transform of the rectangular pulse as described in, is

$$F(\omega) = \text{sinc}\left(\frac{\omega\tau}{2}\right)$$

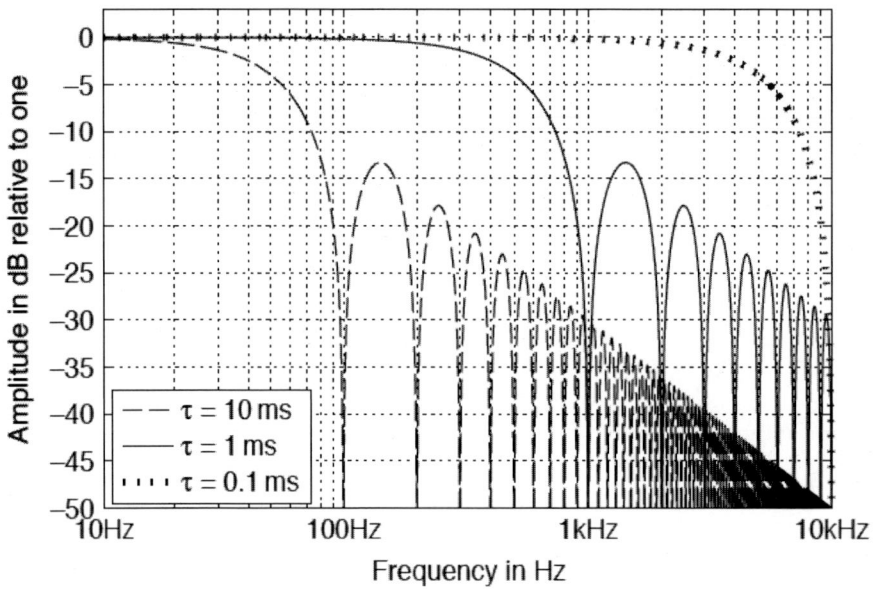

FIGURE 8.5 The spectrum of a single rectangular pulse of length τ for different values of τ

F(ω) is plotted in Figure 8.5 for several values of *Tau*. Note that as *Tau* gets smaller, the frequency extent of the spectrum gets much wider. It is generally true that a waveform which is narrow in time results in a very wide Fourier transform. The converse is also true. In fact, if we reduce *Tau* to zero, giving a pulse of infinite amplitude but still with an area equal to one, the spectrum becomes uniform for all frequencies. This infinitely small pulse is called a *Dirac delta function* and has a uniform—also known as a white—spectrum. It is also sometimes called a *unit impulse*. The only other waveform to have a white spectrum is random noise.

You will notice that the spectrum has points that are zero. These correspond to the frequencies at which one or more cycles are exactly the same width as the pulse. Any components at these frequencies would tilt the flat top of the pulse and hence cannot be present.

NOTES

1. Joseph Fourier, "Mémoire sur la propagation de la chaleur dans les corps solides, présenté le 21 Décembre 1807 à l'Institut national," *Nouveau bulletin des sciences par la Société philomatique de Paris,* no. 1 (March 1808): 112–16.

NINE
Conclusion: Connecting Components

Throughout this book, you have found some "magic numbers" appearing. Table 9 shows how they relate:

$\sqrt{2} = 1.414$	$20 \log 1.414 = 3.0103\ dB$	$10 \log 2 = 3.0103\ dB$
$peak = rms \cdot 1.414$	$peak = rms \cdot \sqrt{2}$	
$\dfrac{\sqrt{2}}{2} = 0.707106$	$20 \log 0.707107 = -3.0103\ dB$	$10 \log \dfrac{1}{2} = -3.0103\ dB$
$rms = peak \cdot 0.707106$		
$\sin 45º = 0.707107$	$\sin 90º = 1$	$\dfrac{90º}{45º} = 2$
$\sin(\dfrac{\pi}{4}) = 0.707107$	$\sin(\dfrac{\pi}{2}) = 1$	$(\dfrac{\pi}{2} \div \dfrac{\pi}{4}) = 2$

Also, one goal of this book is to make connections between simple concepts of frequency, time, and space in order to make a pathway to understanding very advanced concepts, such as Fourier transforms.

Not everyone who reads this book will end up becoming an audio engineer. Of course, if you do consider a career in audio engineering, you will see these concepts at play in much more detail. I hope that you were at least able to make some larger connections and that this text was helpful in laying a foundation for your future efforts in audio and recording.

Appendix A

METRIC PREFIXES

Digital audio commonly makes use of terms with metric prefixes—such as megabytes (MB), gigabytes (GB), and terabytes (TB) for storage. Other frequently used terms are decibels (dB), milliwatts (mW), milliseconds (ms), nanoseconds (ns), or even picoseconds (µs). The specific values for metric prefixes are listed in the table below. (The smaller numbers are useful for measuring jitter.)

Prefix	Multiplier	Decimal Value	English expression
tera	10^{12}	1,000,000,000,000	One terabyte equals one trillion bytes
giga	10^{9}	1,000,000,000	One gigabyte equals one billion bytes
mega	10^{6}	1,000,000	One megabyte equals one million bytes
deci	10^{-1}	.1	One decibel equals one-tenth of a bel
milli	10^{-3}	.001	One millisecond equals one thousandth of a second
micro	10^{-6}	.000 001	One microsecond equals one millionth of a second
nano	10^{-9}	.000 000 001	One nanosecond equals one billionth of a second
pico	10^{-12}	.000 000 000 001	One picosecond equals one trillionth of a second

Appendix B

SOLUTIONS TO THE EXERCISES

Exercise 1-1

Use the radians column when solving for terms using π, and use the degree column when using terms that have the degree symbol (°).

sin x, where x =	y = (DEG)	y = RAD
Π		0
π/2		1
270°	-1	
45°	.707	
π/4		.707
(3π)/2		-1

Exercise 1-2

(a) $\dfrac{\pi}{2} =$

$$\dfrac{\pi}{2}$$

$$\dfrac{3.142}{2}$$

$$1.571$$

133

(b) $\dfrac{3\pi}{2} =$

$$\dfrac{3 \times \pi}{2}$$

$$\dfrac{3 \times (3.142)}{2}$$

$$\dfrac{9.426}{2}$$

$$4.713$$

(c) $\dfrac{\pi}{4} =$

$$\dfrac{3.142}{4}$$

$$0.786$$

Exercise 1-3

1. Given five resistors in parallel all with a value of 10 Ω, what is the total resistance?
Solution:

$$R_T = \dfrac{1}{\dfrac{1}{R_1} + \dfrac{1}{R_2} + \dfrac{1}{R_3} + \cdots + \dfrac{1}{R_n}}$$

$$R_T = \dfrac{1}{\dfrac{1}{R_1} + \dfrac{1}{R_2} + \dfrac{1}{R_3} + \dfrac{1}{R_4} + \dfrac{1}{R_5}}$$

$$R_T = \dfrac{1}{\dfrac{1}{10\Omega} + \dfrac{1}{10\Omega} + \dfrac{1}{10\Omega} + \dfrac{1}{10\Omega} + \dfrac{1}{10\Omega}}$$

$$R_T = \dfrac{1}{\dfrac{5}{10\Omega}}$$

$$R_T = \dfrac{10}{5} \Omega$$

$$R_T = 2\Omega$$

Exercise 1-4

Solve the following equation to find RT in a circuit with two branches of resistance where R1 = 5Ω, R2 = 10Ω, and R3 = 10Ω.

Solution:

$$\frac{1}{\frac{1}{R_1 + R_2} + \frac{1}{R_3}}$$

$$\frac{1}{\frac{1}{5+10} + \frac{1}{10}} \Omega$$

$$\frac{1}{\frac{1}{15} + \frac{1}{10}} \Omega$$

$$\frac{1}{.0667 + .1} \Omega$$

$$\frac{1}{.1667} \Omega$$

$$5.9988 \; \Omega$$

Exercise 1-5

What is the data rate for 5.005 channels of audio recorded at 48 kHz and 24 bits?

$$data\ rate = \#\ channels \times sample\ rate \times \frac{bits}{sample}$$

$$data\ rate = 5.005 \times 48{,}000 \frac{samples}{second} \times 24 \frac{bits}{sample}$$

$$data\ rate = 5.005 \times 48{,}000 \frac{\cancel{samples}}{second} \times 24 \frac{bits}{\cancel{sample}}$$

$$data\ rate = 5.005 \times 48{,}000 \times 24 \frac{bits}{second}$$

$$data\ rate = 5{,}765{,}760 \frac{bits}{second}$$

$$data\ rate = 5.765\ Mbits/sec$$

Exercise 1-6

Given the data rate of a DVD-Video disc is 10 Mbits/second, can it accommodate 5.005 channels of audio at 48 kHz, 24 bits?

Answer: Yes. 5.765 Mbits per second is within the 10 Mbits/second capability of DVD-Video. Keep in mind, this is without regard for video: in reality, the requirements of the video will necessitate finding a lower bit rate for audio. DVD-Audio discs in the early part of the 21st century were an example of a high-quality, audio-only surround format (as were Super Audio CDs (SACDs) which used the DVD format).

Exercise 2-1

(a) Determine how to find power using only current (I) and resistance (R) without using volts (V). Ohm's Law is defined as:

$$V = IR$$

and the power law is:

$$P = IV$$

In order to eliminate the volts term in the power equation, substitute ($V = IR$)

$$P = I(IR)$$
$$P = I^2R$$

(b) How much power is dissipated in a circuit where a 120 V source produces 4.8 amps across a 25 Ω resistor?

$$P = IV$$
$$P = 4.8A \times 120V$$
$$P = 576W$$

Because we also have a term for resistance, we could solve the problem this way:

$$P = I^2R$$
$$P = 4.8^2A \times 25\Omega$$
$$P = 576W$$

APPENDIX B

Exercise 3-1

a. 011

Solution:

2^7	2^6	2^5	2^4	2^3	2^2	2^1	2^0
0	0	0	0	0	0	1	1

$$0 + 2^1 + 2^0 =$$
$$2 + 1 =$$
$$3$$

b. 10001110101

Solution:

2^{10}	2^9	2^8	2^7	2^6	2^5	2^4	2^3	2^2	2^1	2^0
1	0	0	0	1	1	1	0	1	0	1

$$2^{10} + 2^6 + 2^5 + 2^4 + 2^2 + 2^0 =$$
$$1024 + 64 + 32 + 16 + 4 + 1 =$$
$$1{,}141$$

c. 11111

Solution:

2^7	2^6	2^5	2^4	2^3	2^2	2^1	2^0
0	0	0	0	1	1	1	1

$$2^3 + 2^2 + 2^1 + 2^0 =$$
$$8 + 4 + 2 + 1 =$$
$$15$$

Exercise 4-1

Graph of points (-4,3), (-5, -5), (5,3) and (2, -1)

Solution:

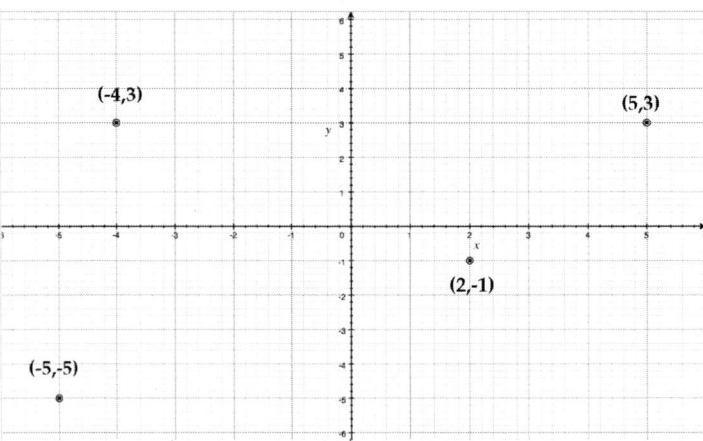

Exercise 4-2

a. Solution:

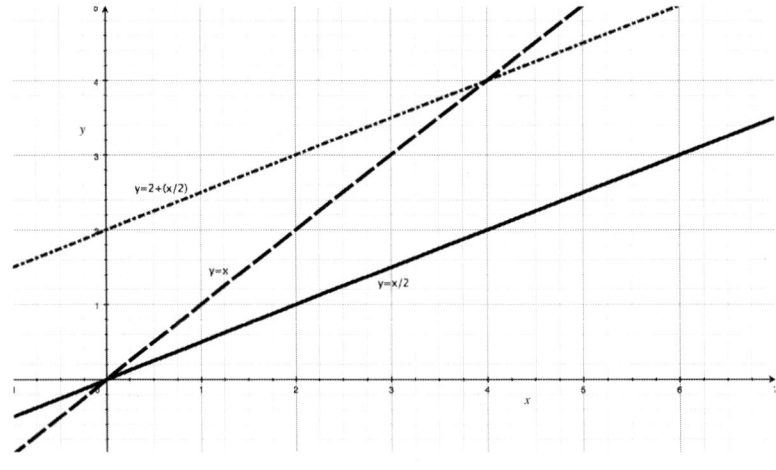

Figure B.2 The graph of $y = x/2$

b. Solution:

$$y = \frac{x}{10}$$

Figure B.3 The graph of $y = x/10$

Exercise 5-1

Given that $fc = 3{,}000$ and $Q = 2$, find the upper cutoff frequency using the equation:
Solution:

$$f_{upper} = f_c \left(\sqrt{1 + \frac{1}{4Q^2}} + \frac{1}{2Q} \right)$$

$$f_{upper} = 3000 \left(\sqrt{1 + \frac{1}{4 \cdot 2^2}} + \frac{1}{2 \cdot 2} \right)$$

$$f_{upper} = 3000 \left(\sqrt{1 + \frac{1}{4 \cdot 4}} + \frac{1}{4} \right)$$

$$f_{upper} = 3000 \left(\sqrt{1 + \frac{1}{16}} + \frac{1}{4} \right)$$

$$f_{upper} = 3{,}000 \left(\sqrt{1 + 0.0625} + \frac{1}{4} \right)$$

$$f_{upper} = 3{,}000 \left(\sqrt{1.0625} + \frac{1}{4} \right)$$

$$f_{upper} = 3{,}000 \left(1.030776 + \frac{1}{4} \right)$$

$$f_{upper} = 3{,}000(1.280776)$$

$$f_{upper} = 3{,}842.328$$

Bibliography

SOURCES CITED

Davis, Gary, and Ralph Jones. *The Sound Reinforcement Handbook.* 2nd ed. Milwaukee, WI: Hal Leonard, 1989.

Fourier, Joseph. "Mémoire sur la propagation de la chaleur dans les corps solides, présenté le 21 Décembre 1807 à l'Institut national." *Nouveau bulletin des sciences par la Société philomatique de Paris,* no. 1 (March 1808): 112–16.

Jones, Pete R. "What's the Quietest Sound a Human Can Hear? (A.k.a. 'Why Omega-3 Fatty Acids Might Not Cure Dyslexia')." Dr. Pete R. Jones's website, 20 November 2014. http://www.ucl.ac.uk/~smgxprj/public/askscience_v1_8.pdf.

Pusateri, Bob. "Signed Integer Ranges: Why and How." *Bob Pusateri: SQL Server and Kindred Subjects* (blog), 26 February 2015. http://www.bobpusateri.com/archive/2015/02/signed-integer-ranges-why-and-how.

Women's Audio Mission. http://www.womensaudiomission.org.

RECOMMENDED READING

Books

Ballou, Glen. *Handbook for Sound Engineers: The New Audio Cyclopedia.* 2nd ed. Indianapolis, IN: H. W. Sams, 1991.

Bartlett, Bruce, and Jenny Bartlett. *Recording Music on Location: Capturing the Live Performance.* Boston: Elsevier Focal Press, 2007.

Huber, David Miles, and Robert E. Runstein. *Modern Recording Techniques.* 8th ed. Burlington, MA: Focal Press, 2013.

Rumsey, Francis, and Tim McCormick. *Sound and Recording.* 6th ed. Burlington, MA: Focal Press, 2013.

Savage, Steve. *The Art of Digital Audio Recording: A Practical Guide for Home and Studio*. New York: Oxford University Press, 2011.

Online Resources

The Physics Classroom. "Sound Waves and Music." http://www.physicsclassroom.com/class/sound.

Sengpiel Audio. "Personal Search Engine." http://www.sengpielaudio.com/Searchengine.htm. (Note the website sengpielaudio.com is in German; use the link above to access the tools in English.)

Index

A
AC *see* alternating current
alternating current [AC] 58–59
AND, OR, and NOT gates 79
angular frequency 119, 124
angular velocity 105, 106
antilogs 73–74
automatic delay compensation 33
average *see* mean

B
bandwidth 18
binary 77

C
capacitive reactance 37
capacitor 61
Cartesian graphs 83, 107
circle 93
   circumference 93
   radius 93
compression ratios 67–70
   knee 69
   threshold 70
compressor 67–68
coordinates 82
current 56

D
DC *see* direct current
decibels 71
degrees 9–10
   on a calculator 9
   graphing 10
delay time *see* time delay
Dirac delta function 128

direct current [DC] 123
distance, solving for 27
DVD-Video 36

E
error 113

F
filters
   low pass filter 63
   high pass filter 62
   peak filter 98, 101
Fourier, Jean-Baptiste Joseph 119
frequency 44
frequency spectrum 122

G
geometric mean 97, 100

H
Hertz 44

I
impedance 59
inductor 59
inverse square law 95

L
latency 30
LFE [Low Frequency Effects of Low Frequency Extension] 35
limiting 70
logarithms 7–8
   On a calculator 7
logic gates, *see* AND, OR, and NOT Gates 79

143

M
mean 109

O
Ohm's Law 56, 59
omega 105

P
pascal 71, 73
    microPascal 71
PCM [Pulse Code Modulated] 76, 111
period 44
periodic function 119
phase 33, 122
polar graph 90
polar plot 91
power 57
precedence effect 34
probability density function 113

Q
Q [Quality Factor] 17, 98
quantization 111

R
radians
    on a calculator 9
    graphing 10
    and circles 15
rate, solving for 27
resistance 18, 56
    solving with a calculator 19
    solving with a spreadsheet 26

resonant frequency 66, 98
RMS [Root Mean Squared] 75–76, 109–12

S
sigma 119
signal-to-error ratio 111
signal-to-noise ratio 111
simple circuits 18
sound pressure level 38
speed of sound 41, 42, 45
sphere 72, 94
substitution 58

T
tau 125–26, 128
time delay 27
    and microphones 28
    and loudspeakers 49
    and bpm 54
time, solving for 27
trigonometric values on a calculator 8
two's complement 79

V
voltage 56
volume (geometrical) 96, 97
VU [Voltage Unit] 74

W
waveform display 87, 88
wavelength 42